Denis Tye

A VILLAGE SCHOOL

Boughton Monchelsea 1850-1970

 **PROTOTYPE, SITTINGBOURNE, KENT.**

8272

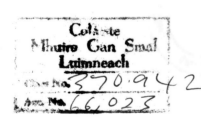
Designed, typeset, printed and bound by Prototype Origination & Print Consultants Ltd, 62 Bell Rd,
Sittingbourne, Kent.

Production details

Typeset in Baskerville face on a Compugraphic Editwriter Series. Text paper 90 gsm machine coated matt
art. Cover board 290 gsm Astralux one sided board. Perfect bound to open flat.

The editor, and Prototype Ltd, would like to point out that the quality of some of the illustrations are not up
to our usually high standard of reproduction, this is due to the poor quality and ageing of the originals.

ISBN: 0 9508047 0 3

CONTENTS

LIST OF ILLUSTRATIONS

PREFACE

It is extraordinary how much rich material on life in the past can still be quarried from documents and other sources, as well as through tapping the memories of those still alive. This study of a fairly typical, rural elementary school is a case in point.

Using the school's log books, which had to be kept by headteachers from 1862, as well as a rich variety of other sources, Denis Tye has succeeded in reconstructing life as it was lived by teachers and pupils in Boughton Monchelsea over a century ago. From about 1900 the story is filled out with the actual memories of pupils who had been at the school in their childhood. For the most recent period the author, who has been head of the school since 1955, is able to base his account on his own memories and knowledge, as well as using oral evidence from others.

This is social history of the best sort. The imposition of compulsory education was not greeted with tremendous enthusiasm by those whose families had for centuries organised their lives according to the rhythm of the agricultural year (in which children played a key part). Quoting aptly from the log books, Mr. Tye shows how long it took until fetes or holidays, ceased to decimate the school as a result of pupils staying away to help at home, in the fields, or for other reasons. The log books also highlight many other serious difficulties schools and schoolteachers had to face over the last 100 years – epidemics ravaged the school, snow and heavy rain made the long walk many had to undertake impossible; then there were the problems of nutrition (or lack of it), physical defects, and the like.

In this history, the author charts the gradual emergence of easier conditions; as also of radical changes in the curriculum and in the use of more humanist teaching methods – the last consequent on the slow decline in the size of classes and the employment of properly trained teachers. He records the changing status of the school, its transformation from a Church school (in its origins) to one maintained by the School Board (and later the local authority); its reorganisation more recently, the move to establish close contact with parents and the life of the community generally.

It is a fascinating story; told with verve and flair; a valuable contribution to the history of education. but one which will be of special interest not only to the community served by the school (now well into its second century) but to all concerned with social history. In this book, voices speak from the past, but with an immediacy which is seldom achieved in historical writing.

Brian Simon
Professor of Education/University of Leicester

Acknowledgements

Without the invaluable help of many former pupils, parents and staff of the school, a book of this kind could not have been written. there are, for example, extracts from tape recordings made by no less than thirty-two different people, not to mention more than a score of letters. I would like to express my warmest thanks to them all.

I am indebted, also to Sybil Marshall, author of An Experiment in Education, Leonard Marsh M.Ed., Principal of Grosseteste (Teacher Training) College and R.O. Oblitas, O.B.E., ED., M.A. formerly of H.M. Overseas Civil Service, who read the first manuscript and advised, very perceptively, what needed to be done to make it attractive to the general as well as to the local reader. But I owe most to John Birtwhistle M.A., Lecturer in English Literature, University of York, who, as editor, brought to bear his talents as a writer and his knowledge of education in its wider social and political setting to craft a very attractive work-box out of an over-stuffed school chest.

I am very appreciative of the generous preface from Professor Brian Simon, a foremost authority on the History of Education.

I am grateful to Allison Wainman and Tony Brown of Prototype who have taken great pains to produce a very attractive looking book; to Pat Nossek and Angela Kleiser who typed the first and second manuscripts, to David Millar and Alan Cocks for help with reproducing copies of old photographs, Don Howe for cover 'slate' calligraphy and Brian Higbee for technical advice.

And, finally, my thanks to the Kent Education Committee, not only for allowing me to use the School Log Books but also, for twenty-six years, permitting one... slightly eccentric village schoolmaster to get on with his job with the minimum interference.

Denis Tye

Chapter I: 1850 – 1872

Vaguely like a church, the school walls were built of ragstone eighteen inches thick. The roof was high-pitched and showed its rafters to the classrooms. The windows were high up in the walls, lest pupils be distracted. All you could see out of them were the tops of trees. In summer, the barred windows were whitewashed, to keep out the sun. The woodwork was dark brown varnish, the walls bare – except for a map or print of Biblical theme. The lamps were oil, the heating smoky coal. The children wrote on squeaky slates rested on their knees. A wood and frosted-glass partition stood between the Infants' room and the other Standards, clustered not by age but according to some idea of ability. The Infants' room had a gallery at the back and up there near the window it was cold.

The Master's house was on the north side and it eschewed a damp course. Every morning he rang the bell at five minutes to nine. Every morning, at nine o'clock, he locked the door.

The foundations for that establishment were laid in 1850 at Boughton Monchelsea, a small village south of Maidstone in Kent. I have described the village, and assembled the memories of some older inhabitants, in *A Village Remembered*. [1] In the present little book, I shall follow the progress of the school up to the time when I was headmaster but it was otherwise a more cheerful place. The quest for its history has taken me from Diocesan records to local newspapers; from old photographs to living memories; from the County Library to a black tin trunk stowed in a farmhouse and labelled sombrely 'SCHOOL BOARD'.

So much of what we should now love to know was never recorded because 'records' are kept by a narrow band of society for its own purposes. Some, even of records such as these, are lost. A volume of the Log Book is suspiciously missing. Early school records were destroyed in the 1832 fire at the parish church or the 1942 'Baedeker' blitz on Canterbury. From about 1890, however, not only are the records richer but I have been able to enliven them with the taped reminiscences of old people in the village. [2]

Obviously, the fascination of this quest for me has been firstly that I know the place and the people and am convinced that such memories are of intense value to a local community. I cannot hope, however, to convey this fully to the general reader. Too much of its texture – for example, the sense of particular families continuing through the story – can be fascinating only to participants. Yet there is a deeper interest still, in attempting to trace the threads of national change that are entangled in the particulars of one village's experience. For example, in the sacking of a headmaster in 1890 we shall discern a whole system of causes then placing education under strain. A school is a marker of society. It carries out its changes and shows what they mean for the individual.

– 2 –

And before the ragstone edifice with its chilly gallery? A Sunday School on record from 1818. Then a weekday and Sunday School in some cottage, supported by subscription and the children's pence. Also a number of private or dame schools for the custody, rather than education, of their charges. It is with that building of 1850 that education was really established in the village of Boughton Monchelsea – and the reason is national.

The Education Enquiry of 1833 disclosed that out of every ten children four did not attend school at all. Three went to Sunday School, and two went either to very inefficient dame schools or to the private variety. With these findings, Education was about to receive its first government grant, but it was not yet to be state education. Both the Royal Lancastrian Society, established in 1810 by Joseph Lancaster to build Nonconformist Schools, and the National Society for the Education of the Poor, established in 1811 to build rival Anglican Schools, were to receive £20,000 to meet half the cost of building school houses. There was still reluctance to build state schools as such, or to favour either Society at the expense of the other. We can now see the building of Boughton Monchelsea Parish School by the National Society in 1850, as a point in the rivalry to build

END. ELEVATION OF SCHOOL.

END. ELEVATION OF HOUSE.

PRINCIPAL. ELEVATION.

MARCH. 25th 1850.

W. G. & E. HABERSHON.
ARCHITECT
3A BLOOMSBURY SQ.

Architects Plans for the National Society School of 1850
Architect W. G. & E. Habershon. Bloomsbury.

[3]

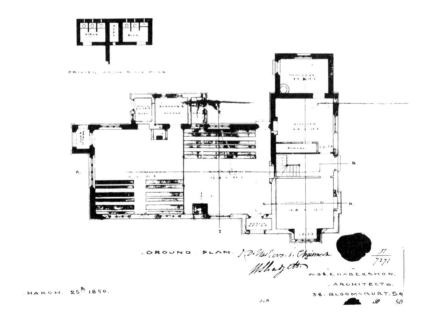

Nº 122.

SCHOOLS AND SCHOOL HOUSE &c.

BOUGHTON MONCHELSEA

KENT.

CHAMBER PLAN

GROUND PLAN

W. G. & E. HABERSHON,
ARCHITECTS.
38. BLOOMSBURY, Sᵠ

MARCH. 25ᵗʰ 1850.

schools that followed the dispensation of 1833.

When the Reverend M. Jefferies, applied to the National Society for aid towards erecting a school, he prudently claimed that there was no existing provision for education in the parish. The building he proposed was to consist of two rooms, 22' × 21', with accommodation for 75 of each sex, thus allowing six square feet per child. The site was the gift of the squire of Boughton Monchelsea Place and main landowner in the district, Thomas Rider Esquire. The cost of school and schoolmasters's house amounted to £609 and 6 shillings, of which half had been raised locally. The Education Department's grant was £114, the Dioscesan Education Office allocating £75 and the National Society £45.

It was anticipated that the teachers' salaries and other costs would amount to £90 per annum and it was proposed to charge twopence per child per week for instruction and to rely on subscriptions for the remainder. By 1852, there were 125 children attending the school, run as it was by Mr. and Mrs. Crook.

– 3 –

In 1839, the Crown was persuaded to set up a Committee of the Privy Council to 'consider all matters affecting the education of the people.' The first education department was thus established by Royal Prerogative and not by Act of Parliament. The first secretary, Dr. Kay (later Sir James Kay-Shuttleworth), was one of the pioneers in English education. He perceived – whilst he could not eradicate – the weaknesses of the prevailing 'monitorial' system of class teaching. This system had been instituted on the advice of Dr. Bell, head of the National Society, who had instructed huge classes in India by using a system of monitors – older pupils acting as untrained assistants at negligible cost.

Dr. Kay's successor as Secretary to the Council, Robert Lowe, was an educator of a different kind. It was his intention to apply to this art certain 'economic' theories of which we hear from time to time. 'Hitherto', he declared, 'We have been living under a system of bounties and protection. Henceforth we propose to have a little free trade.' In answer to fierce criticism he unveiled his Philosophy of Education: 'If it is not cheap, it shall be efficient, if it is not efficient it shall be cheap.'

The outward and visible sign of this profound attitude was the 'Revised Code' of 1862, which laid down that grants to schools would be dependent upon two variables:

> *Children's attendance at School, and an annual examination by an inspector in Reading, Writing and Arithmetic (hereafter, 'the 3 R's').*

This system of 'Payment by Result' was destructive for children and teachers alike. It demoralized teachers because their livelihood depended on grants that could only be earned by the pupils; and the Code narrowed the curriculum to the subjects that would be examined. References to inspection and examination fill the Log Books:

> *Needlework too much confined to one style. Singing very good. The fifth standard are not too perfect in some of the tables and the reading is too low and indistinct.*

Or, in plain English, the children mumbled and there was the same obsession with learning tables that we find a century later.

– 4 –

Those quotations are from the School Log Book,[3] which is far-and-away the most important source of information we have for the early years. Local and professional historians have recently 'discovered' these logs to be a unique and fascinating source of information.[4] When I arrived at the School, I found its log books thrown into a box on the hall floor. As they were kept continuously from 1863, they go back further than most and give us a full and vivid record of children, teachers, parents and school visitors; but more – they relate the school to village life and show how class divisions and social attitudes outside were reflected within the classroom.

As local historians, we have this much for which to thank the reviled Revised Code – that under it the department of education enforced the keeping of such log books, although cautiously stipulating that 'no reflections or opinions of a general character may

_1866._

Hail to another year —
The year that now begins!
All hail to him who led us here
Through dangers & through sins!

Jany 1. A beautiful day — quite a contrast from yesterday, which was so wet and windy that we could not get to Church. The Vicar called this morning. 22 Present this evening. Scripture lesson — Lot's choice.

2 Nothing particular to record.

3 The reading in the 6th class is, I think, very fair, & I have no doubt will be good enough to fulfil the requirements of the R. Code; but it will be impossible in the time to get through the reading book, the latter part of which is extremely difficult. Present this evening 23. Scripture lesson — Lot rescued by Abram —

4 Ordinary progress.

5 The progress made during the week has been upon the whole satisfactory. But the spelling in the 3rd & 4th classes requires

Probably sung at Thanksgiving Service on rebuilding the Church after the fire of 1832.

HYMN,

TO BE SUNG BY THE CHILDREN,

OF THE

Boughton Monchelsea
PARISH SCHOOL,

ON SUNDAY, MAY 18, 1834.

I.

O would you wish on earth to know
In heavenly breasts what spirits glow;
'Tis Charity—whose sacred flame
From Heaven's eternal altar came.

II.

O would you wish on earth to view
God's holy Image, bright and true;
'Tis Charity—whose radiant vest
For Christ's own Banquet decks the guest.

III.

O would you live in hope serene,
And close in hope, life's transient scene;
Let Faith and Charity supply
The spring, and Hope shall never die.

IV.

Faith, Hope, and Charity, "these Three,"
In heart unite, in toil agree;
One Spirit feeds, one Law defines,
One blessing cheers, one Soul combines.
HALLELUJAH! Amen.

PRINTED BY J. BROWN, KENT ARMS OFFICE, 87, WEEK STREET, MAIDSTONE.

[8]

be entered?

> *The Principal Teacher must daily make in the Log Book the briefest entry which will suffice to specify either ordinary progress or whatever other facts that may deserve to be recorded. My Lords are of an opinion that a zealous and intelligent teacher will not be at a loss to make other entries and will **not** find the term 'ordinary progress' expresses the whole of his experience from year's end to year's end.*

The retort of William Lockyer Banks, headmaster – called 'schoolmaster' – at Boughton Monchelsea School, was swift and pointed:

> ***July 9th 1863.** As I claim to be 'an intelligent teacher' I am bound to take up Mr. Lindgren's glove. My answer is four-fold:-*
> 1. *I do not desire to keep a log book.*
> 2. *A log book is not a private journal.*
> 3. *It often happens that the surest progress is least noticeable.*
> 4. *'Let another man praise thee and not thine own mouth.'*

Nevertheless, he soon found a ringing style for the job. His first entry reads:

> *Non nobis, domine, non nobis; sed Nomine Tuo da gloriam, Amen.... I lay this the first Stone of my 'Honourable Monument.' Wm. L. Banks.*

Could it be that his independence of comment was not unconnected to his impending retirement?

> *The school will re-open under a new master as I remove to Birchington for the benefit of my children's health. This, therefore, is my last entry.*

Banks' successor, John James Ares, could be just as grandiloquent on occasion. An early entry declares the man:

> *With an earnest desire to impress that knowledge which is peace and to lead the young to the fountain of life, I commence the work and labour of love again.*

[9]

The high moral tone, varied only by facetiousness, runs throughout his entries:

Ellen White discharged for insubordination and neglect of duties
(This entry noted also the 'gentlemanly' manner of the inspector.)

Most splendid rewards were given this afternoon to all that passed the Inspector's examination last March; also rewards for regular attendance at Sunday School. A Magic Lantern was exhibited afterwards and the children were highly delighted with the entertainment and their rewards.

A person found an umbrella belonging to one of the children and very honestly brought it to school this afternoon.

G. Gilbert was very insolent to me this afternoon; gave him a good caning. Prov. XIII24.

John James Ares would never use a short word where a long one would suffice: the weather is 'inclement', the boy 'insolent', a magic lantern 'exhibited'.

-5-

The standard of attainment, nationally, was low. As late as 1880, only a quarter of the pupils qualified for a grant on examination in the 3 R's. At Boughton in 1864, of the 97 who dared attend that day, only 59 were offered up for examination and in the end only six qualified for the grant. The standard, however, soon rose at this school. In 1886, the Inspector reported:

	£	s	d
49 boys and girls presented for examinationl			
Passed in Reading 47 grant	6	5	4
Passed in Writing 47 grant	6	5	4
Passed in Arithmetic 44 grant	5	17	4
Under 6 years of age 5 grant	5	17	4
Average attendance 64	12	16	0
Total Grant	£ 32	16	0

Children stayed away from school for a variety of reasons.

Sometimes the parents could not afford or refused to pay the school 'pence' or needed their children as wage-earners at home, as in these entries.

> *Mrs. Potter refuses to pay 2d for her son's schooling.*
>
> *The Olivers and Wenbournes owing a week's schooling and refusing to pay, were suspended this morning.*
>
> *Augustus Hubbard left today. His mother requires his services at home.*
>
> *Mrs. Godfrey called to say she had obtained a situation for Henry and should be obliged to take him from school; she also wanted Elizabeth at home. She was very pleased with their progress and regretted having to take Henry from school.*

The attitude of the schoolmaster to parents is typified by this entry of 1865:

> *Mrs. Oliver came to school to complain about her children being punished for stealing and lying (so much for the 'co-operation of parents').*

And again the sarcastic phrase echoing, perhaps, a department order stressing the need for same:

> *This afternoon his father sent me a short abusive letter threatening to take him from school if punishment was inflicted again. So much for the 'co-operation of parents'.*
>
> *Arthur Thomas played truant again today. An incorrigible boy, but, doubtless, his father is to blame.*

We are made also aware of the great hazards faced by children from the accidents and eqidemics of rural life at the time. In 1865, 'Charles Bennett is ill with the fever'. In 1866, an infant is reported to be seriously ill: 'She was frightened by Mr. Shadgett's horse running away. The doctor gives but faint hopes of recovery.' In 1868, another meets with 'a sad accident' when 'meddling with a turnip-mill': he had his fingers cut off. In 1869, another is reported ill with fever, and three days later *John Colvin died on Saturday. Rev. XIV. 3.*

There are few references to the outside world, which seems to have extended about as far as Maidstone, the nearest town. When, in 1863

> *Two schoolmasters from the South Coast admired my plan for teaching long-division both simple and compound*

the South Coast seems as far away as the Ivory Coast. Rather, we sense the excitement of local events which were in their own way complex.

> *A cricket match in Mr. Moore's Park, a Sale by Auction at the Brewery and a Fair Day at Loose – hence only 70 children in school.*

In 1869, the first penny readings took place in the village schoolroom in the evening.

> *A reading from 'Nicholas Nickleby' by W. Moore Esq. and then a song by Mr. Rodwell brought forward Mr. J. Hayes who much amused the company by a selection from 'Handy Andy'.*

There were more reading, songs and a piano duet, whereupon

> *The National Anthem closed a very interesting evening. The room was crowded by an audience who loudly cheered those who took part in the programme.*

Then there was Sunday School:

> *Mrs. Burr came this morning to know the reason George did not have a Sunday School ticket this morning. A very good reason why, because he was not at school – played at truant.*

And, for the more ambitious, Evening School:

> *Wm. Sunnucks and James Brooker left the Evening School. As*

This Indenture made the *first* day of *June*

18*54*, between *Emma Wagon* of *Aylesford*
of the first part; *John Wagon* of *Aylesford* of the second part,
(* *father* of the said* *Emma Wagon*
Edward Garrard Marsh of *Aylesford*
and * *John Wickham Barnes* of *Aylesford*
William Kirkby of *Aylesford*
(* *managers* of the *Aylesford Educational Society's* school), of the third part,
and * *Maria Anne Nash* of *Aylesford*
(* *Mistress* of the said* *Aylesford Educational Society's* school), of the fourth part;

WITNESSETH that the said* *Emma Wagon* of h*er* own free will,
and with the consent and approbation as well of the said* *John Wagon*
as of the said* *Edward Garrard Marsh*
John Wickham Barnes
and *William Kirkby*

doth hereby place and bind h*er* self apprentice to the said* *Maria Anne Nash*
to serve h*er* henceforth until the 31st day of December, 185*9*, (inclusive) in h*er* business of a School *Mistress*
in the * *Aylesford Educational Society's* school aforesaid.

AND in consideration of the acceptance by the said* *Maria Anne Nash*
of the said* *Emma Wagon* into h*er* service, and of the covenants
on the part of the said* *Maria Anne Nash* hereinafter contained, the
said* *John Wagon* doth hereby for h*im* self, h*is* heirs, executors and
administrators, covenant and agree and the said* *Emma Wagon* doth promise
and engage with and to the said* *Maria Anne Nash* h*er* executors, administrators
and assigns, that the said* *Emma Wagon* shall at all times during the said term
faithfully and diligently serve the said* *Maria Anne Nash*
in h*er* business of a School *mistress* in the * *Aylesford Educational Society's* school aforesaid, and shall not,
except from illness, absent h*er* self from the said school during school hours, and shall conduct h*er* self
with honesty, sobriety and temperance, and not be guilty of any profane or lewd conversation or conduct,
or of gambling or any other immorality, but shall diligently and obediently assist in the instruction and
discipline of the scholars of the said* *Aylesford Educational Society's* school, under the direction of the
* *mistress* , and apply h*er* self with industry to the instructions which shall be given h*er* by the
* *mistress* , and shall regularly attend divine service on Sunday.

AND for the considerations aforesaid the said* *John Wagon*
doth hereby, for h*im* self, h*is* heirs, executors and administrators, further covenant with the said*
Maria Anne Nash h*er* executors, administrators and assigns,
that he the said* *John Wagon* h*is* executor*
and administrators, shall at all times during the said term provide the said* *Emma Wagon*
with all proper lodging, food, apparel, washing, medicine and medical attendance.

AND in consideration of the covenants and agreements hereinbefore contained on the part of the
said* *John Wagon* and* *Emma Wagon*
* he the said* *Maria Anne Nash* doth hereby for h*er* self,
h*er* heirs, executors and administrators, covenant with the said* *John Wagon*
h*is* executors, administrators and assigns, and also as a separate covenant with the said*
Emma Wagon h*er* executors, administrators and
assigns, that * he the said* *Maria Anne Nash* shall at all
times during the said term, or so much thereof as *s* he shall continue *mistress* of the said school, to the
best of h*er* ability teach the said* *Emma Wagon*
the business of a School *mistress* as carried on in the said school, and afford h*er* daily opportunities
(Sundays and the usual school holidays only excepted), of observing and practising the art of teaching in
the said school, under the superintendence of h*er* the said* *Maria Anne Nash*
and devote one hour and a half at the least in every morning or evening, before or after the usual hours of
school keeping (except as aforesaid), to the further personal instruction of the said*
Emma Wagon in the several branches of useful learning usually taught in the said

---

Insert in the place where the undermentioned number occur particulars according to the following directions:—

No. 1.—The Name of the Pupil Teacher.
2.—The Name of Father or Mother, or other relative or friend, who is a party to the Indenture.
3.—The Names and Residences of a quorum of the Committee of Managers, if there be such a Committee; and if not, then the Names of the Trustees or other persons in whom the School and School Premises are vested.
4.—The Name of the Parish or District, and whether the School is a National or a British School, thus:—"*Fulham National School,*" "*......... British School.*"
5.—The Name of the Master or Mistress.
6.—Here insert "Trustees" or "Managers" as the case may require.
7.—Here insert "Master" or "Mistress" as the case may require.
8.—Plural.
9.—Here insert "Father,"—"Mother," if a widow,—the degree of relationship of any friend.

N.B.—The Father, if alive, is to be a party to this Indenture. The Mother is to be a party only when the Father is dead,
and another relative or friend only when the Apprentice is an orphan.

Pupil Teachers Emma Wagon's Indenture of Contract

Fees payable for pupil teachers attending Central Classes in Maidstone.

Central Classes for Pupil Teachers.

All Saints' School, Maidstone.

The Treasurer of *Boughton Monchelsea* Schools

to the Central Classes.   Dr.

	£	s.	d.
Matthew Wm. S. 3 Terms	1	1	0
Edmed Ellen 1 Term		7	0
Kitham Kate 1 Term		7	0
	£1	15	0

Kindly remit this amount to

M. Leecher
All Saints' School
Maidstone

IMPORTANT

TO

PARENTS AND EMPLOYERS OF CHILDREN.

Act to Regulate the Employment of Children in Agriculture (5th August 1873).

This Act comes into full operation on the 1st January 1875.

Its provisions should be complied with by sending children to school during the year 1874 who will be under 12 years of age at the close of it ; since otherwise they cannot be employed in agricultural labour during 1875.

After January 1st, 1875, no employer, or his agent, may employ any child under 8 in agricultural labour, unless he be its parent or guardian, and then only on land in his own occupation.

After January 1st, 1875, no employer, or his agent, may employ any child over 8 and under 12, unless the parent or guardian can produce a certificate [which will be in force for 12 months from its date] to the following effect :—

If the child be over 8 and under 10, he must have completed 250 school attendances (that is, 25 weeks at least,) within the 12 months immediately preceding the issue of the certificate.

If he be over 10 and under 12, he must have completed 150 school attendances (that is, 15 weeks at least,) within the same period. (N.B.—No children, whether boys or girls, can be excepted from these rules but those who have passed the 4th Standard.)

No child under the age of ten years shall be employed in any agricultural gang.

Morning school and afternoon school each count as one attendance.

The school must be a school recognised by Government as efficient, if there be one within 2 miles of the parent's home.

Every employer (that is, any person occupying not less than one acre of land), or agent of an employer, guilty of an offence against the Act shall be liable to a penalty of £5.

Any other person committing an offence against the Act shall be liable to a penalty of £1.

But no penalty shall be inflicted for employing children above 8 years of age during School Holidays, or temporary Closing of the School—

Or in Hay Harvest, Corn Harvest, or gathering of Hops; and the Magistrates have the power to entirely suspend the Act during a few weeks in the busy seasons of the year.

[Copies may be obtained at the rate of 1s. per 100, on application to the Secretary, National Society's Office, Sanctuary, Westminster.]

Employment of Children Act 1873.

[14]

soon as the Scripture Lesson was over each took his cap and went his way. They said they wanted to learn to read and write and not to hear about Scripture. . . I believe they are gone to Mr. Gandy's School where they can do that which is right in their own eyes

-7-

A noticeable omission during this period is any reference to other teachers. We presume that the Ellen White who in 1864 was discharged for 'insubordination' was a monitor. In 1863, on the first page of the Log Book, we have the first reference to pupil teachers. These had to be at least thirteen years old and had to have passed an annual examination conducted by the inspectors. Queen's Scholarships, by competition amongst pupil teachers and tenable at training colleges, were designed by Kay to supply trained recruits to the elementary schools. Specimen questions from the late 1880's would be:

Write full notes of a lesson on one of these subjects –
(i) (for infants) The square and its properties (either by paper folding or drawing)
(ii)Adverbs and Adverbial phrases

Arithmetic *(males)*
(i) Find the square root of 5,294,601
(ii) A man bought 240 cows at a foreign port paying £12.6s. for each and 128 sheep at £1.17s.6d. per sheep. Their carriage to London amounted to $\frac{1}{24}$ of the price paid for them: he then exhanged them for 221 ponies, which he sold at £17 per head. What did be gain on this expenditure?

Domestic Economy *(needlework)*
Name and describe all stitches used in completing:
(i) a woman's nightdress or
(ii) a full-size flannelshirt
State the quantity of material required for each and its cost. [5]

The training colleges were the first to be hit by the Revised Code of 1862, which reduced their grant, their numbers (by reducing the number of Queen's Scholars) and their standards. The numbers dropped from 14,000 in 1861 to 9,000 in 1866.

The indenture for a pupil teacher at another school in 1854 promises that the headmistress

> *will give Emma Wagon daily opportunities to observe and practise teaching and devote one hour and a half at the least every morning or evening before or after the usual hour of teaching to the further personal instruction of the said Emma Wagon in the several branches of useful learning usually taught in the said school.*

The burden that this placed on the head-teacher will become clear in the entries from 1870 onwards.

-8-

With the first great education act of 1870, Boughton Monchelsea School ceased to be a National School and became a Board School. **The 'Forster Act'** aimed to complete the voluntary (that is, religious) system,

> *sparing the public money where it can be done, and procuring as much as we can the assistance of the parents.*

This was still not yet state education, but the government had understood that the voluntary bodies would be unequal to the task of providing all the extra schools or enlarging the existing schools to cater for the fast-growing population.

New Local authorities, the School Boards elected by ratepayers, were set up 'to repair the deficiencies', that is to fill in the gaps which the voluntary bodies could not cover. And for the first time, primary education was to be compulsory. The Byelaws for Boughton Monchelsea, as for other schools, imposed on parents that they 'shall cause' children between five and thirteen to attend school on pain of summons to

> *a meeting of the School Board, to give your reasons why your child does not attend school as aforesaid. And, herein, if you fail, you will be liable to be proceeded against according to the law.*

[16]

Schooling was not, however to be free of charge. Although the 'pence', so often mentioned in the Log Books, could be remitted in case of extreme poverty, the fee was to cause great hardship and, together with families' need for work or wage from their children, was the reason for much absenteeism and early leaving.

> *In the countryside, local voluntary effort normally sufficed to provide any extra accommodation.* [6]

and in the Canterbury Diocesan Report of 1873, the Reverend B. Smith reports:

> *I can only recall to mind one transfer of a Church School to a School Board in the past year.*

That single transfer was probably the school at Boughton Monchelsea, for in 1871 its premises were leased to the School Board at a peppercorn rent. The school remained a Board School, the peppercorn rent was rescinded only in the 1960's, and the Church still has the right to free use of the school after 5 p.m. and at weekends. This may well explain the conviction of many older people that, in their time at least, it was a Church School; and also, something of the Vicar's attempts over the decades to intervene in school life – so that as late as 1959 the log reads:

> *The Vicar voiced disapproval of the fact that Mrs. McLaren was a Catholic teacher but I assured him that the children would be safeguarded from any doctrinal teaching.*

But why should Boughton have made this unusual passage from Church to Board School? It appears that a meeting of the School Committee and ratepayers quarrelled over architect's plans for the enlargement of the school; and the diocesan records show that a grant form sent to the vicar for this purpose was never returned. Between November 1870 and March 1871 this, and perhaps other divisions which it symbolised, dragged on until

> *March 1st 1871. A meeting was held in the schoolroom, by the ratepayers for the purpose of passing a resolution that it is expedient*

that a School Board be formed.

The first elected Board consisted of a maltster, a retired miller, two farmers and a butcher.

-9-

In an Inspector's report of 1870, Mr. Ares is depicted as

a hardworking conscientious teacher, but he seems to me to need some assistance.

This is credible, for to train his pupil teachers he began work at 7 a.m. and had then to supervise pupil teachers and monitors all day long. His day ended with teaching Evening School.

At the beginning of 1872, Ares records

school very full. 131 children on the registers and only one monitor to assist.

He calls on the Lord for help, and certainly little enough was forthcoming from 'My Lords' of the Department of Education. The census of 1871 showed that in what we should now call Ares' catchment area,

there are 273 children belonging to tradesmen and labourers between the ages of 3 and 13; 46 between 3 and 5, and 227 between 5 and 13.

The poverty of many in this category is confirmed by repeated references to charity. For example,

Mr. J. Hayes called to ask if the church wardens could use the schoolroom on Saturday to give out the annual charity of calico and flannel

and later, in 1871,

The Clerk to the School Board brought some calico to be made into shirts and shifts.

A Miss Taylor, daughter of Boughton Place, is recorded as donating copy books to the higher classes. The difficulty in paying the pence is illustrated in the entry:

Admitted Caroline King at half the usual school fee by order of the School Board.

It is hardly surprising, then, that William Burr for example is taken from school by his mother and set to work:

he may be considered to have left school: He is 11 years of age and not able to read.

In spite of the School Board bye-laws there seems to have been no attempt to keep such a child at school.

In 1871 the first caretaker, Mrs. Lamb, was appointed 'to sweep the schoolroom and light the fires'. Hitherto parents had often complained of their children set 'to sweep the schoolroom'. The first fires were lit well into the winter, and the coal was ordered just half a ton at a time.

Of these early years we do not have the vivid personal impressions that come later; but it is tempting to wonder whether Goldsmith's lines in *The Deserted Village* do not apply far beyond his 'Sweet Auburn':

Beside yon staggling fence that skirts the way,
With blossom'd furze unprofitably gay,
There, in his noisy mansion, skill'd to rule,
The village master taught his little school;
A man severe he was, and stern to view;
I knew him well, and every truant knew;
Well had the boding tremblers learn'd to trace
The day's disasters in his morning face;
Full well they laugh'd, with counterfeited glee,
At all his jokes, for many a joke had he;
Full well the busy whisper, circling round,

Convey'd the dismal tidings when he frown'd;
Yet he was kind; or if severe in aught,
The love he bore to learning was in fault;
The village all declar'd how much he knew;
'Twas certain he could write, and cypher too;
Lands he could measure, terms and tides presage,
And e'en the story ran that he could gauge.
In arguing too, the parson own'd his skill,
For e'en though vanquish'd, he could argue still;
While words of learned length and thund'ring sound
Amazed the gazing rustics rang'd around,
And still they gazd, and still the wonder grew,
That one small head could carry all he knew.

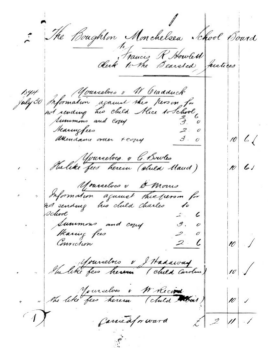

Fines imposed on Parents at Bearsted Petty Sessions for their childrens
non-attendance. 1894.

Chapter II: 1872–1890

-10-

The story of the next headmaster was unfortunate in a way that tells us much about the conditions of education at the time. With the appointment of Ayres to a private establishment at Wookey Hole, the school at Boughton passed to Albert Rolfe. He was a certificated master trained at Culham, a Church of England Teacher-training College for men. His inspector's report of 1881 was satisfactory ('tone and order very good'), even though no other details are logged save a reference to the need for the boys and girls 'offices' (lavatories) to be separated. The last entry in this volume is for April, and the next volume is missing or perhaps was never-written up.

The next we have opens in March 1889. Her Majesty's Inspector hints at what may have been going on by reporting that

> the work in general is free from some of the egregious faults of some former years. A successful attempt has been made to improve attendance.

In the manner of inspectors, he finds something with which to balance his judgement:

> The maps drawn, however, were mostly worthless and the proper names somewhat remarkably ill-spelt.

Next year, however, his tone is more grave:

> I was much in hopes that the relative improvement shown last year was a sign that the school was about to resume a sound and good position.

[21]

A few subjects are singled out as 'fairly taught', but

> *When this has been said, there is nothing else in the school that*
> *merits commendation and much that calls for adverse comment.*

The inspector goes on to specify weakness and ends by threatening the school's grant:

> *Having regard to the antecedents of this school and the previous low*
> *level of attainments, I can recommend no Merit Grant. A school*
> *where so much of the attainment is so low as it is here, is not doing*
> *the work for which a Public Elementary School exists.*

The duplicate letter book of the School Board shows a prompt flurry of correspondence between vicar and squires. The last example of epistolary art informs Albert Rolfe that these gentlemen have

> *unanimously resolved, very reluctantly, to call upon you to tender to*
> *them at once, your resignation of the office of headmaster or teacher,*
> *such resignation to take effect three months from the date hereof.*

That Rolfe made some reply is attested by the following cryptic note to him:

> *Dear Sir,*
> *   I am in receipt of your letter of yesterday's date. I confess I do not*
> *understand the tenor of it. Will you be so good as to explain to me*
> *what is meant by the words 'it is informal' contained therein?*
>
> > *I remain,*
> > *Yours faithfully,*
> > *George Hunn, Clerk to the Board.*

Notice that Mr. Rolfe is addressed as 'Dear Sir' and the letter ends 'Yours faithfully', whereas the letters to the Board members begin 'Sir' and end 'Your faithful servant' or 'Your obedient servant'.

The post was advertised in **The Schoolmaster** and **The School Guardian,** salary £100 a year:

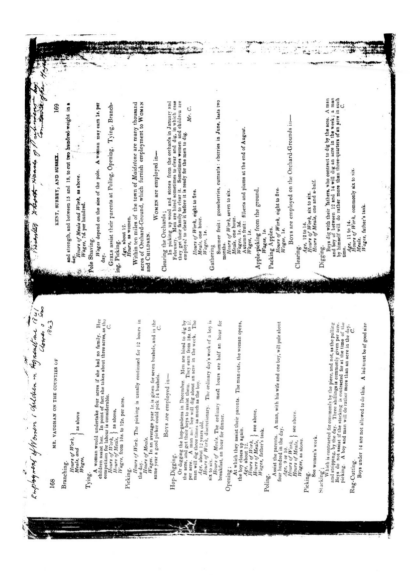

Branching.
Hours of Work, and Meals, and Wages,} as above.

Tying.
A woman would undertake four acres if she had no family. Her children assist her. In point of fact she takes about three acres, as the competition for labour is considerable.   C.
Hours of Work, } as above.
Hours of Meals, }
Wages, from 10s. to 12s. per acre.

Picking.
Hours of Work. The picking is usually continued for 12 hours in the day.
Hours of Meals.
Wages. In an average year it is given for seven bushels, and in the same year a good picker could pick 14 bushels.   C.

Boys are employed in—

Hop-Digging.
Or digging the hop-gardens in December. Men are hired to dig by the acre, and get their boys to assist them. They earn from 18s. to 1l. per acre. A man and boy will dig about an acre in the week. The man will dig three times as much as the boy.
Age, about 12 years old.
Hours of Work, discretionary. The ordinary day's work of a boy is six to six.
Hours of Meals. The ordinary meal hours are half an hour for breakfast, an hour for dinner.

Opening.
At which they assist their parents. The man cuts, the woman opens, the boy closes up again.
Age, about 12.
Hours of Work, } see above.
Hours of Meals, }
Wages, father's task.

Poling.
Assist the parents. A man, with his wife and one boy, will pole about four hundred in the day.
Age, 9 or 10.
Hours of Work, } see above.
Hours of Meals, }
Wages, as above.

Picking.
See women's work.

Stacking;
Which is contracted for commonly by the piece, and not, as the pulling and stripping, by the day. Three shillings is commonly given per acre. Boys do not assist if the stacking is contracted for at the time of the picking. A boy and man will do rather more than an acre in the day.   C.

Rag-Cutting.
Boys under 14 are not allowed to do this. A lad must be of good size

and strength, and between 15 and 18, to cut two hundred-weight in a day.
Hours of Meals and Work, as above.
Wages, 7d. per hundred.

Pole Shaving.
Wages depend on the size of the pole. A woman may earn 1s. per day.

Picking.
Girls assist their parents at Poling, Opening, Tying, Branching, Picking.
Age, about 12.
Hours, as women.

Within ten miles of the town of *Maidstone* are many thousand acres of Orchard-Ground, which furnish employment to WOMEN and CHILDREN.

WOMEN are employed in—

Clearing the Orchards;
In picking up wood and stones from the orchards in January and February. Men are hired sometimes to clear and dig, in which case they get their family to clear it. Sometimes women and children are employed, to clear it before it is ready for the men to dig.   Mr. C.
Hours of Work, eight to five.
Meals, one hour.
Wages, 1s.

Gathering
Summer fruit: gooseberries, currants: cherries in June, lasts two months.
Hours of Work, seven to six.
Meals, one hour.
Wages, 1s. 3d.
Autumn fruit: filberts and plums at the end of August.
Wages, 1s.

Apple-picking from the ground.
Wages, 1s.

Packing Apples.
Hours of Work, eight to five.
Wages, 1s.

Boys are employed on the Orchard-Grounds in—

Clearing.
Age, 12 to 14.
Hours of Work, six to six.
Hours of Meals, one and a-half.

Digging.
Boys dig with their fathers, who contract to dig by the acre. A man and boy of between 12 and 14 will dig an acre in the week, a man by himself will do rather more than three-quarters of an acre in such time.   C.
Age, 11 to 14.
Hours of Work, commonly six to six.
Meals.
Wages, father's task.

Pages from Employment of Women and Children in Agriculture 1841 presented to both Houses of Parliament by Mr Vaughan

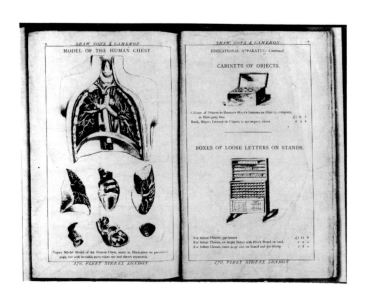

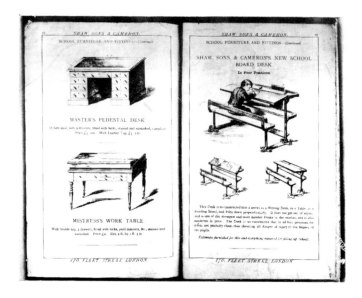

Pages from catalogue of Educational Apparatus C1890.

*The wife of the Master will have to teach gratuitously the girl pupils
plain sewing daily for one hour and a half.*

Rolfe inscribed the log:

August 19th 1890 *School dismissed for the Hop-picking
vacation. Headmaster leaves today after 18 ½ years service. This is
my last entry. Thank God I've done my Duty.* **Quocumque
Trahunt Fata Sequamur.**

-11-

What are we to make of this story? The immediate cause of
dismissal is clear, and to the inspector's report should perhaps be
added several letters and minutes in which Rolfe is called upon for
financial information. There was no suggestion of dishonesty, but
some of inefficiency. The deeper causes, however, are suggested in
the handling of Rolfe's dismissal. This displays both the socially
inferior position of the headmaster and the complete insecurity of his
office.

What was the status of the elementary teacher? In 1889 a
headmaster wrote:

*I am well aware that even yet there are great differences of opinion
regarding the amount of education to be expected from an elementary
teacher. Some persons seem ever afraid lest the poor be educated
beyond their station.* [7]

The social definition of the elementary school teacher still reflected
that of the separate system of which is formed a part. Early attempts
to create some form of Registration Association to make teaching one
of the liberal professions were not for teachers in elementary schools.
This was true of Bills defeated in 1869, 1879 and 1881. The first
attempt to draft a Bill including all teachers was in 1890, one of the
promoters being the National Union of Teachers.

We should understand the social isolation and low social status of
headmasters like Albert Rolfe. He was not regarded as the

professional equal of the doctor, parson and lawyer. Teaching was one of the few avenues open to working class men and women to gain entry to the lower middle class, whereas other professions were, in the main, educated at public schools. Even so, it is striking that the schoolmaster should be the servant not only of the local squire and the local farmer on the School Board, but of the local butcher as well. At the same time, the village schoolmaster would be isolated from the other subordinate orders of society. He tended to be contemptuous of the parents of the the poorer children in his charge. He was often disliked and feared by the poorer parents for preventing children going to work, and for his inevitable rejection of their complaints. His employment was completely in the hands of the Board who could summarily dismiss him if ever his Results reduced the grant from the Department of Education.

Relics of this system survived well into this century. Indeed there are traces, particularly in the isolated rural areas, today. When I was interviewed in 1955 for the present head-mastership, the vicar questioned me, quite illegally, about the frequency of my churchgoing. For years afterwards. at every managers' meeting, then held in the vicarage, I had to sit on a dining chair by the door whilst the managers sat round the room in easy chairs.

-12-

Let us go back to the beginning of Albert Rolfe's 'mastership'. Each successive headmaster cries out at the abysmal standard of work in the school bequeathed to him. Thus, in 1872, Mr. Rolfe is writing in the Log Book:

> *I find two classes of the school backward in everything. I thought an extra monitor quite necessary and therefore engaged F. Shadgett on my own responsiblity.*

And soon:

> *Out of the 40 children neglected last year by the last master, 25 are now fully up to standard.*

His main instrument of improvement was the cane. The

admission of his own son, aged 3 years and 6 months, did not soften his views, for the said Frederick is soon beaten for inattention. Within a week he was caning Henry Mortimore 'for not attending to his reading'. Certainly one senses his determination to assert his authority quickly, particularly over unruly boys. An extraordinary entry, in October 1872, announces that there would be 'No talking allowed in future in school'. We gasp at the impracticability of such an edict and conclude that Mr. Rolfe's lack of confidence in his powers must have been responsible.

November 5th *I find the school much better under strict discipline.*

But on November 6th, we read that the admirable Ernest Thompsett was caned for talking.

Next, he records that

> *I find the boys much improved in their behaviour owing to the practice of drill in playtime.*

and finally:

> *Orders were given last week that no child would be admitted after the bell had rung, and the door would be locked punctually at 9 and 2 o'clock. Bertha Lettham, George Trowel and Edmund Folly punished for going home on finding the door locked at 9.5.*

From 1872 to 1882 we sense the strain of imposing these disciplines – and remember Mr. Rolfe had a school roll of about 190 and only two qualified assistants. This strain was responsible for unenforceable rules and probably to the master's ill-health. Thus, in February 1873, 'suffering from a gathering in the head', and in November of the same year: 'The work seems very heavy this morning. I am troubled with my head'. In July 1874 he records: 'Master suffering with acute pains in the head and face caused by excessive heat and the draughts'. The continuous strain of over work – the master's day began with pupil-teachers' lessons at 7 a.m. and continued on into evening school – the constant pressures to maintain good attendance and to get children through the annual examination, must have imposed an intolerable burden.

We get the sense that discipline, particluarly with the boys, must have rested on a knife-edge and guess that there were many unruly boys from the poorer homes and for whom school had no attractions, who must have posed a continuous threat to the master's authority. Just take one log book entry; that a monitor was chosen to report the broken windows **daily**.

Boys, particularly, were caned for a wide variety of misdemeanours such as:

> *beating on the black board with a rough stick*
> *smoking a pipe in the playground*
> *talking too much over lessons in the dinner hour*
> *breaking an umbrella handle to use as a hoop stick*
> *breaking a window with a nip – cat (i.e. a cap 'bomb')*
> *throwing turf at the carriages for Miss Braddick's wedding as they passed the school. (Miss Braddick was the daughter of the Chairman of the School Board.)*

Other 'crimes' included stone throwing, insolence, truancy, trespassing on a field of mustard, and stealing – not sweets, but turnips. Here are entries relating to the theft of school property (which might have been rewarded for the interest it showed in learning):

> *Punished Bedwell for putting slate pencils in his pocket instead of the box kept for them.*
> *Punished Silas Ashdown for taking alphabetical letters away from school. Mrs. Ashdown called and tried to shield her boy by blaming Harry Boyce; after a deal of pro and con, I quietly left her at the door and went to work.*

In 1877, the Master 'missed two reading books and sent for three small locks from Mr. Woods to put on the teachers' desks'.

Then we have several pictures of 'posses' of children tearing round the countryside to bring back truants:

> *Had trouble with Jn. Mannering. His mother brought him to school but soon afterwards be went missing. Alfred Godfrey and*

Jesse Baker were sent after him. As he objected to walk, they tied his legs and carried him.

Chown F., a very bad boy generally, spends his schooling (his 'pence'). Sent two boys almost to Pested, who caught the celebrity reposing in the shade of a gooseberry bush.

Master absent half an hour to find Fryman who had played truant. Traced him through the Quarry and finally landed him in school.

The teachers and monitors copied all too readily the master's example in beating children. In 1872 we read 'the master cautioned the teacher for striking the small children'. A pupil teacher recently 'failed' at Inspection for sticking pins into the children: 'The master finds no less than 12 children had suffered from the pin-pricking'. Consequently, we find the master instructing the pupil teachers on 'Modes of Punishment'.

-13-

As with the moral tone of Banks and the verbosity of Ares, the punitive mentality of Rolfe is hard to discriminate from the style of his times. To be set against it are a few references to 'school treats' and 'a concert in the school to raise money in aid of the Boughton Excursion Fund' – the excursion being to the Crystal Palace which had been set up for the Great Exhibition of 1850. For those unable to go to the Palace of iron and glass, there was another 'exciting treat':

After school the little ones sat down to a comfortable tea in Pond Field. After amusing themselves, each child had a toy and some sweets to go home with.

And one summer the Master

gave all the children in school some ripe cherries for attending school on Fete Day. (The Grand Amalgamated Fete in Linton Park.)

In 1873 Mr. Rolfe gave a supper to the Night School, but 'I took

[29]

the cane from my desk in the night school to keep order'. Again, he records: 'Night School now getting troublesome'. Night Schools, which began in the 1860's, were often to be found in village schools, varying greatly in numbers from county to county. All too often the children were too tired with chores at home or the labours of the day to resume battle with the 3 R's. The fee was usually 2d a week and some early school-leavers did go back and learn to read.

These were positive and perhaps even effective responses to need. I suggest that the insecure and primitive side of Rolfe had to do with the professional insecurity I have outlined. This combined with the work ethic of the time – a spirit expressed by the Log Books in the hard metaphor of industrial revolution. Whilst the curriculum dealt with 'The Railroads of England', the children were to be driven as though by the same forces. Thus in 1877, 'children better up to their work owing to steam pressure in the earlier months'.

The school had to keep up this pressure in the face of a poor attendance rate which closely related to the community still being rural and backward. When the headmaster speaks of the children 'leaving their learning in the fields', it is more than a complaint at their idleness in class. It is also an admission that agriculture was indeed an informal system of knowledge, and the modern school had not yet suppressed the 'truancy' of this learning in favour of its own curriculum which was later to incorporate a neat vegetable patch on school premises.

-14-

At the time, however, the reluctance of the rural and backward culture to travel 'the Railroads of England' presented itself as a range of disparate problems. These included epidemics, inadequate clothing and footwear when young children walked in all weathers to school, the difficulty of poor families affording the pence, the pressures to get children out of school and into 'gainful employment', and truancy, often triggered off by some local fair, fete, agriculture show or bonfire.

To take epidemics first: an entry of 1877 may stand for many in which mumps, measles and scarlet fever vie with carbolic powder:

One case of fever reported from Coxheath in the Chambers family. As the day was fixed for the Foresters Fete I thought it was a fit opportunity to have the schools thoroughly disinfected. Mr. Cleaver (Inspector) called at 9 o'clock and after going through his performances, all ventilation was stopped, and the schools kept closed till the following morning. When the school was opened – every place seemed sweet and healthy. I think with care and Mr. Cleaver's assistance we may prevent the spread of the disease in the Parish which otherwise would necessitate the closing of school for weeks.

Other absences were caused by inadequate footwear and clothing in winter. The roads, before tarmac, were thick with mud in winter and dozens of children of all ages walked two or three miles or more to school, often returning home at lunch time for there were no school meals. This explains why the afternoon session did not begin until 2 o'clock.

In 1873 the burden of fees was exacerbated by an increase from 2 pence per child to:

4d per week for the 1st child
2d per week for the 2nd child
1d per week for the 3rd child
1d per week for all infants
1d per week for all children of widows

this in the days of large families and of farm wages at no more than 10 shillings a week. After 1873 there are many references to the burden:

Had plenty of trouble with parents and children alike about the pence.

In 1875, Mrs. Noakes sent word by Emily that she could not pay more than 6d for her four children, Emily, Caroline, Alice and Alfred, and 'if I could not take them for that, I was to send the children home'. In the same year; 'Potter's children admitted at a reduced rate on account of his death'. (In 1868 Mrs. Potter had refused to pay the pence.) An example from 1878 shows the quandary:

Jane Maynard still persists in not bringing 4d for her school fees. I have sent her home 3 or 4 times and sent messages to her mother but the child is still absent.

We can also read of the pressures to get children out of school and into work so as to supplement family income: 'William Woollet gone bird minding'. Bird-scaring boys were paid pence – remember **Jude the Obscure** – but boys in school had to bring their pence.

Fruiting had commenced in earnest and no doubt for a week or two a number of children will be absent.

Truancy does not seem to call for much explanation. What child would not prefer an agricultural show, a fair or bonfire, to going to school? This kind of event, however, is to be seen as part of the weave of agricultural life which included the other factors of poverty and child labour. The celebrations of the agricultural year – even, on one occasion, a demonstration of agricultural labourers – were the other side of its work; and children's participation in them was therefore not quite the same as modern truancy.

-15-

Nor could the response of a school to one or other form of non-attendance be what it is now.

Foresters Fete today at Boughton Mount. Very few children present. School dismissed when the band passed.

The 1870 Education Act, so important and yet inadequate, made further legislation on attendance inevitable and this was vigorously demanded by the National Education League and The T.U.C. In contrast to the Boughton Monchelsea School Bye-laws of 1872, which laid down attendance from 6 to 13, only 450 out of 2,000 School Boards had in 1880 adopted bye-laws enforcing attendance. In that year, however, such bye-laws were made obligatory. An Act in 1891 enabled Boards and Voluntary Schools to admit children free and claim compensation.

4ᵗʰ December 1891.

At a Meeting of the Boughton Monchelsea School Board held on Friday the 4th day of December 1891 in the Board School.

Present

John Willraham Braddick Esqᵈ Chairman
Mr. Frederic Smith   Vice Chairman
and Mr. M.A. Atkins.

The Minutes of the last Meeting were read and confirmed.

Reported the Balance in the hands of the Treasurer £ 18.11.3.

The following Accounts were presented and it was resolved to pay the same

	£	s	d
W. J. Latham — Advertising in "Schoolmaster" for Infants Mistress		1	6
A. M. McIntosh — Infants Mistress — Travelling expenses		2	
Educational Supply Classes 14ᵗʰ c/e	11	13	
George Colman — Coal a/c	1	0	
Edgar Button — Draper a/c	4	11	2
J. R. Forder — Principal Teacher	4	13	10
2 mos Saly. to 30ᵗʰ Nov. 1891			
Incidentals for month ended do		1	5
Mrs Seager — Cleaning a/c	1	16	
9 weeks ended 27. Nov. 1891			
Kate Latham — Monitress		13	6
9 weeks Saly. ended ditto			
William Goodhew . Monitor		10	6
7 weeks Saly. ended ditto			
Carried forward £	14	19	9	£20 . 1 . 2

Page from Minute Book of Boughton Monchelsea School Board 1891.

Education Department circular on Pupil Teachers.

CIRCULAR TO H.M. INSPECTORS.

Instruction of Pupil Teachers (Art. 34).

Circular 343.

EDUCATION DEPARTMENT,
WHITEHALL, LONDON, S.W.
6th January, 1894.

SIR,

My Lords have observed with regret that a large number of Pupil Teachers fail to obtain a place in the Class List for the Queen's Scholarship or are placed too low to be qualified for entrance into a Training College. They have reason to believe that this low standard of attainments proceeds in many cases from the neglect of School Managers to see that their Pupil Teachers are carefully and regularly taught.

The following regulations have been laid down by Their Lordships for the future guidance of School Managers, and any serious disregard of them, after due warning, may lead to the disqualification of the School as a place of proper training for Pupil Teachers (see Article 34 of the Code). The regulations do not apply to cases where the Pupil Teachers attend efficiently conducted Central Classes.

(1.) The hours in which instruction is given should be entered on a Time Table, and the Managers should ascertain by a personal visit, at least once a quarter, that the hours are properly observed, and should record their visits in the Log Book, or other book kept for the purpose.

(2.) The time should not be spent in private reading, but in actual instruction by the Teacher.

(3.) As a rule the instruction should not be given between the morning and afternoon meetings of the School except for a short part of the winter season, neither should it be given immediately after the afternoon meeting except under very special circumstances. A reasonable interval of time should be allowed between the afternoon meeting and the instruction in all cases where it is given in the latter part of the day.

(4.) The Managers should provide good reference books and text books for the use of the Pupil Teacher, such books to remain the property of the School, and to be approved by the Inspector at his annual visit.

(5.) Note books and exercise books used by the Pupil Teacher should be shown to the Inspector at his annual visit. All exercises and notes should be dated by the Pupil Teacher when they are written, and dated by the Teacher when corrected.

(6.) A book should be kept for the purpose of recording the Pupil Teacher's progress in skill in the conduct and teaching of his class. Short notes of lessons on one of the subjects prescribed by the Code for Pupil Teachers' apprenticeship, and in the last two years full notes of lessons should be prepared weekly in the first two years of apprenticeship, and in the last two years full notes of lessons should be prepared weekly in the presence of the Principal Teacher. A report on such notes and on the delivery of these lessons in the last two years should be made weekly in this book.

(7.) Quarterly examinations should be held by the Teacher or some other qualified person in each subject of the Pupil Teacher's course for the year, and the worked papers, after being marked by the Teacher, should be submitted to the Managers with a short report upon them, and subsequently produced to the Inspector at his annual visit.

I have the honour to be,
Sir,
Your obedient Servant,
F. T. Kitchins

To
H.M. Inspector of Schools.

The Grange
Blandington
Chester
24.11.99

Dear Sir

Having seen your advt. for a certificated Assistant Mistress, I beg to offer myself as a candidate for the post. I am 29 years of age, and have passed the first and second year Certificate Examination. I was a Pupil Teacher in Holy Trinity Infants Sch Cheltenham, where I afterwards served 4 years as Assistant Mistress.

On 1891 I was appointed Assistant teacher in charge of the Infants Department (under a Master) of Wrexham Church School, with an average of about 200. I received my teachership whole at the school. In 1898 I was appointed Head Mistress of the Infant Department of the Cathiot Church School Grade D Cheltenham, which position I relinquished in 1899 as it did not succeed in raising my certificate in order to superintend Pupil Teachers.

For the last six months I have been in St Peters School Greenwich S.E., but resigned the post in September and have not been in actual service.

I can play the piano and have a good knowledge of music. I am also intimately acquainted with the Kindergarten system.

I have very good health and have not been away from school for illness more than a month during the last four years.

Trusting you will give my application favourable consideration.

I am
yours faithfully
Edith Maud Walker

Letter of application for Teaching Post at Boughton Board School 1899.

But, until 1891, legislation was one thing, enforcement quite another – especially in country areas where magistrates were often sympathetic to the farm-workers who kept their children away from school and to the farmers who wanted the children's labour. The Agricultural Children's Act of 1873 was intended to improve attendance, but the fines imposed by the magistrates were often derisory. After 1890, however, the attendance officer became quite formidable and is very well remembered by old people to whom I have spoken in the village.

Two significant facts stand out in the period 1870 to 1900. First, that the population rose from 22 million to 32 million and secondly, there was a change in the climate of opinion about education. This, together with the abolition of the school pence in 1890, had most effect on school attendance. for example, in 1890, an official report commenting on changes in attitude since 1870 observes:

> *the value of a good school has become more widely appreciated and parents evince an increasing desire to secure the benefits of efficient teaching for their children.*

The growth of literacy, reflected in the tremendous growth in demand for popular literature, both indicated this changed attitude and helped to shape it. For the years 1871, 1881 and 1891, the Registrar General gave the national literacy rate for males as 80, 87 and 94% and for females as 73, 82 and 93% respectively. Charles Dickens rose to fame on the back of this growth in literacy.

-16-

To meet its new role in an industrialising England, the school needed not only to enforce attendance but also to revise its curriculum and improve its teaching. The difficulties are clear from Mr. Rolfe's continual bother with his pupil teachers, whom he had the duty of instructing at seven o'clock, a.m.

> *Weston not able to leave his bedroom and I find the work most heavy.*

> *Pike seems to lose courage with Algebra and can't properly*

understand 'Stocks'.

Pike departed the same year to be master of the school at Coxheath Workhouse, where the ability to calculate stocks and shares was even less urgent.

Nationally, the pupil teacher system was coming under increasing attack for putting immature and inefficient apprentices in the classroom and giving them extremely poor instruction.

> *Until the end of the century pupil teachers were recruited at thirteen or fourteen (the age was raised to 15 in 1900). They did some twenty hours of teaching a week. Demands for secondary education for pupil teachers were one of the main pressures towards the expansion of the scholarship ladder and the system of secondary schools.* [8]

-17-

In March 1875, we find Rolfe struggling with a new curriculum:

> *Commenced hard work in all classes. How I am to get through all the work for the various standards since the alteration in the Code adds Geography, Grammar and Literature to the 3 R's – I am at a loss to know.*

What was this all about? The Revised Code of 1862 had forced schools to narrow the curriculum to the grinding of the 3 R's, examined annually; plus needlework and cloth-cutting for girls and drill for boys.

After 1870, there was some relaxation of the Code and schools could earn extra grants for 'specific subjects' in addition to the 3 R's. In 1871 a grant of 3 shillings was introduced for each child successful in an examination in not more than two such subjects, which included geography, history, algebra, geometry, the natural sciences, political economy, languages – 'or **any** definite subject of instruction. . . taught according to a graduated scheme'. [9] Only about 2-3 per cent of children were presented for 'specific subjects' in the 1870's but, under the 1875 Code – of which Rolfe made such heavyweather – so called 'class subjects' were introduced. Grants for these were made to schools on the basis of proficiency classes, not the examination of individual children. The Code of 1882 was to add a standard VII for grant-earning examinations and introduced a classification of schools as fair, good and excellent with three corresponding levels of merit grant.

In the next few years the National Union of Elementary Teachers (to become, in 1889, the National Union of Teachers) would campaign successfully against the remaining features of 'payment by results'. In 1891 this system was undermined; general inspections without notice replaced inspections on an appointed day. 'Absurd and mischievous' deductions from the grant were ended and the system abandoned by which 'the worse the school was, the more the means of improving it should be taken away'. But a small element in the grant per child was still made dependent on an inspection examination.

At any rate, by 1878, Rolfe had adjusted to the change and 'the children also passed creditably in the class subjects geography and grammar'.

-18-

Some of the more interesting Log Book entries at this time concern an innovation called 'the Object Lesson'. As we might suspect from the way this phrase has passed into the language, a single object would be taken in its various aspects as a starting point for larger perspectives of an edifying character. From a practical point of view, however. the object lesson is a particularly English style of empirical knowledge, aptly suited to the horizons of modern labour. That is to say, it combines maximum practical understanding of the object in hand with minimum apprehension of its real context.

The object lesson was criticised as a mental aridity: an Inspector in the 1840's had spoken of infants

> *who knew of pachydermatous animals, and monocotyledonous plants, absurdities which are often witnessed.* [10]

But the first Object mentioned for Boughton Monchelsea, in 1873, was 'The Table'. Later Object Lessons included such richly educational topics as 'The Pin', 'The Window' and 'The Goat'. In the Object Lesson we can see the beginnings of a practical approach that is remembered by a recent pupil:

I remember in one lesson we took the cream from the school milk; we put it into a screw top jar and added salt and pepper, then we passed it round so that each child should shake the jar. We did this until butter had formed and Mrs. Hann spread it on some bread, with jam, for each to try.

(Charlotte Priestley)

In 1896, the obligatory subjects were the 3 R's, needlework for girls, drawing (for older boys), object lessons, or one 'class subject'. In addition schools could provide such 'class subjects' as singing, recitation, drawing, English, geography, science, history and domestic economy. 'Specific subjects' were selected from a long list including mechanics, chemistry, physics, agriculture, languages and shorthand. Girls could be taught cookery and laundry or dairy work, and boys gardening. Explicit provision was also made for manual instruction, physical exercise and visits to institutions of educational value.

The first reference to model drawing occurs in 1877 and a drawing examination is mentioned in 1880: 'Sent returns to Science and Art Departments concerning the Drawing Exams on the 8th of March'. The influence of industry is further shown by an entry in 1881 referring to a lecture

by a Mr. Evans of the Staffordshire Potteries. He made several articles such as cup and saucer, tea-pot, etc. in the presence of the children who expressed their satisfaction by constant clapping of hands. Mr. Evans is no doubt a practical workman and his lecture was thoroughly instructive and amusing.

In 1877 the first reference is made to recitation. 'Began Cowper's "Receipt of his mother's picture" '.

References to singing as a curriculum subject come as early as 1872:

[38]

Class of 1898.

School Football Team 1899.

A. Letham. G. Cole. E. Woolley. J. Ambler. W. Froud. V. Froud. C. Cloak. A. Ashby. P. Bowles. E. Walker. S. Thirkell. H. Sunnucks. S. Ashby.

Attendance Certificate 1912.

School 1910. The front garden used for growing vegetables; background Mr Forder.

Vocal music must, in future, form part of the ordinary School Course of Instruction or the Grant will be reduced at the rate of one shilling per scholar according to the number in attendance.

The ensuing songs were often listed in the Log Book:

God Bless the Prince of Wales
Father Come Sit by Me
Kiss Me, Mother
Under the Willow
Forward Boys
The Song of the Stitch
A Farmer's Boy
Please Give me a Penny, and
Hold up the Right Hand.

On one occasion 'The Vicar called to complain about the nonsensical effect of continuous singing'. His conception of sensible singing might perhaps be represented by this verse from **All Things Bright and Beautiful:**

The rich man in his castle
The poor man at the gate
God made them high and lowly
And ordered their estate.

With teachings like that, it was quite plucky of those eight boys to throw their turves at the wedding carriage of the daughter of the Chairman of the School Board. We salute their memory.

Chapter III: 1890–1923

From now on, a certain loss of colour from the log book is more than compensated by the living memories that I have tape-recorded, and we have a picture of the school and its headmaster from viewpoints other than his own and that of H. M. Inspector. The next headmaster, Philip Robert Forder, was appointed in 1890. His early years are remembered by those over 80, whilst a 65 year-old recalls him as 'a silver-haired gentleman'.

Forder resigned in 1906 to take up the post of Inspector of Biblical Instruction. He withdrew his resignation and stayed on until he retired in 1923. One's impression from the log books that he was a correct man, rather imposing, is confirmed by oral witness:

Tall, six foot, thin, feet stuck out at a quarter to three.

(Ron Costen)

*Very good looking, tall and slim and precise. Very well dressed, down to the last bootlace, and I think **they** were ironed. A bit stiff? Well, you couldn't go up to him and talk to him as I'm talking to you; you'd be shaking in your shoes, wondering if you were going to say something wrong, do you see?*

Nellie Pledger (née. Bolton)

A good teacher and liked on the whole. A bit snooty in some ways, and he had his favourites.

(Dorothy Froud)

I remember once, he used to come in, in the morning. He might be a bit ratty; all of a sudden his old tooth would drop; he'd got one false tooth. If that dropped, we knew we had to be quiet, or else we was for it.

(George Potter)

Temperance Certificate of Merit.

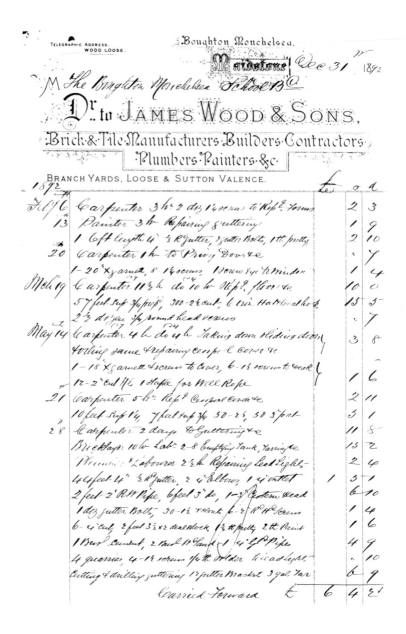

Bill from James Wood & Sons, The Green, Boughton Monchelsea.

He was the organist on Sundays in the church. He was strict on the religious programme in school, first thing in the morning.

(Nellie Pledger)

I was told that his nick-name of 'Old Flick Forder' was because he would flick children's heads as he walked by and found they were not working.

Mrs. Forder, who taught the girls needlework, was petite as her husband was lofty.

He had a very rotten time with her really. You know she wasn't really 'all there'. She used to get on her bicycle, then off she'd get, turn round and come back. He would be following behind her.

(George Potter)

Such a report should be seen against the strains for such an unpaid helper of the school:

My mother was the Infants mistress. Mrs. Forder treated her shameful and, do you know, she had a class of 60 infant children and only a girl of 14 to help her. She had the impudence to bring a whole lot of girls for her to take for needlework. Do you know what my mother did? She walked them right back again and said 'This is your job'.

(Dorothy Froud)

There were two Forder boys:

Both were away in other schools most of the time. One was a proper gentleman, the other was a riff-raff.

(George Potter)

The oldest one came into the school and went to teacher – training college. I don't know what happened to the other – he was the happy-go-lucky one.

(Nellie Pledger)

The standard of teacher – training colleges was now improving and, in some contrast to his predecessor, Mr, P.R. Forder was a well-educated man[11] and something of a scientist. He detailed his accomplishments as follows:

Pupil Teacher in Priory Upper Grade.
Trained St. Mark's College, Chelsea, 1882-3.
Received Parchment 1886.
Certificates held by above:

Drawing Parchment No. 10389
Advanced Sciences

Agriculture	)	
Physiology	)	*First Class*
Magnetism and Electricity	)	
Sound Light and Heat	)	
Physiography	)	*Second Class*
Hygiene	)	
Mechanics	)	

Mathematics Stages 1 and 2 – First Class Archbishops Divinity College Diploma.

And when I asked with whom the Forders would mix, socially:

Not with the village, as such. He'd know the Vicar and he'd know the Miss Smiths and he'd probably go down to see Colonel and Mrs. Winch at Boughton Place. But he'd never have parties or anything like that. He was well known in the village and the parents respected him but the school was his school and he didn't mix very much.
(Nellie Pledger)

The Rolfes would hardly have mingled with Squire and Vicar. We shall see that this difference coincided with a national improvement in the status of education during Forder's period as headmaster; and he was to leave that office considerably strengthened at Boughton.

An assistant teacher, George Bonny, was also appointed in 1890 and – for reasons not obscure – was nicknamed 'Boozer'. When school shut of an afternoon, the headmaster and his wife would take a walk to Glebe Cottage and back: Bonny would make for The Oak. He lived with his mother a mile from the school and on his way every morning he would gather a clutch of children. There is a consensus that he was as round as his bowler hat. He is reported as a kindly man who both allowed himself to be teased and yet could be arbitrary in punishment.

Unaccountably absent from 1887 to 1890, he resigned in 1920. The Log Book reads:

> *The Head Master, after conferring with the staff, has arranged that one member of same shall have charge of the children who bring their dinners, and, also, to exercise general supervision of the school during the dinner interval. Mr. Bonney, however, objects to performing this duty and wishes to resign his appointment*

whereas at the presentation of

> *a silver mounted unbrella and a framed enlargement of the school staff, the latter being a gift especially desired by him*

it was explained that he had retired, as

> *a result of failing eyesight owing to acute rheumatism.*

George Bonny died the day after he retired

> *He used to come round to see your work, for he was a good teacher; he used to get hold of your cheek and pull it hard, like this.*
> **(Dorothy Froud)**

-21-

Staffing was otherwise inadequate and impermanent for most of

Forder's time. There were only three qualified teachers up until 1906, being supplemented by monitors, monitresses, and pupil teachers. All were badly paid, and had to impose a poorly designed curriculum on some very reluctant learners.

Staff and salaries are listed in a School Board Minute book as follows:

£

Mr. P.R. Forder – Head Master   8.8.8. *monthly or £104p.a.*
Mr. Geo Bonny – Cert. Asst.   4.6.8 *monthly or £56 p.a.*
Mrs. A.M. Froud – Infant Mistress 3.6.8 *monthly or £44 p.a.*
William Beeching – Monitor 6 shillings weekly)   *or*
Alice Masters – Monitress 6 shillings weekly) £3.12.0 *annually*
Mary Allchin – Monitress 6 shillings weekly)

In addition the certified teachers received a proportion of the Annual Government grant, which added about £42 p.a. to Forder's salary and £14 to Bonny's. The headmaster's salary was held to include his wife's as sewing mistress. Occasional rises in salary would be negotiated indiviually.

Amongst the particularly ill-paid infant teachers, there were five resignations and a dismissal between 1891 and 1899, and the same again between 1903 and 1918. Reasons given include ill-health (grounds for dismissal), poor teaching, and failure to discipline the class:

> *Had occasion to complain of neglect of the work in the infant room. Both Miss Barker and monitress engaged in conversaion while the children are in disorder.*

> *Miss Barker requested by Head Teacher to confine her attention to the work of teaching and to leave her private knitting at home.*

The H.M. Inspector's report of 1903 commented on the difficulties in the infant's room:

> *The help afforded by a monitress of 14 years of age is obviouly inadequate to secure good training in these large lower classes.*

In 1905, Mr. Forder comments:

Problems of Staffing

With the present staff it is practically impossible for the Head Master to instruct the pupil teachers and monitresses in the art of teaching; also to conduct the periodical examinations in the School.

Two years later,

Headmaster has to teach standards 4, 5, 6 and 7 (80 or so children) in addition to supervising the work of the school.

As for the various monitors, monitresses and pupil teachers, two or three went on to college but nearly all graduated to the farms or domestic labour.

It is in the 1920's that I detect not only a greater stability in respect of staff changes, but an improvement in quality as well. A broadening of the curriculum and a greater participation by the school in the community were all part of the impetus to education that followed the First World War.

-22-

For 30 years, Old Flicker Forder, Boozer Bonny and their assistants kept going a school of 200 pupils between the ages of 3 and 14. It was a period in which rural life hardly seemed to change. The same class pyramid was intact, although the definition of poverty rose a little. To go on to higher education still needed 'money'. And yet the Great War, hardly mentioned in the records of an all-age school, had begun to disrupt the fixed order of All Things Bright and Beautiful. Hardy wrote a poem **In Time of 'The Breaking of Nations'** in which the motions of the old plough-horse were offered as some kind of permanence to set against the War; but at that moment the very farm horses of Kent were being conscripted to the mire of French battlefields. The memorial board of this school, as of so many institutions, records heavier loses than for World War II. Although civilians were not in the front line as in the second war, the strain on fatherless families was acute: the main nourishment for many children came from boiled bones at the soup kitchen on the village green.

Village life was never to be quite the same again. There would still be 'high or lowly', but not in the secure forms familiar to the village.

[49]

The influence of the larger local landowners would decline. There would be a shift from hop and cob-nut growing to fruit farming and chestnut coppicing, and from horse-drawn vehicles to motor tractors. By 'shaking out' labour, each of these changes would accelerate an underlying trend, namely that farm labour and its associated crafts, together with domestic service for women, were no longer dominating local employment. A simple, decisive opportunity would come with the buses that in the 1930's a business man started to run from the village green into Maidstone. These, followed by the motor car, would take young women to the counters and desks of the commercial town, young men to the workshops and garages, and everyone in the village from their dependency on local shops, pubs and clubs – which would steadily close down.

Each major war has been followed not only by social change but also by some conscious movement for social progress and, both to express and to contain these movements, each war brings its Education Act:

> *The Education Acts of 1870, 1902, 1918 and 1944 were passed in time of war, and it would seem that men's minds, in revulsion against the folly, waste and false values of war, turn to education as one hope for the future – though there are not those wanting who are interested in education primarily as a means of promoting military efficiency.* [12]

At the end of the nineteenth century, School Boards were defended by the Noncomformists and Trade Unions as democratic, and attacked by the Conservatives in opposition as expensive and as divided in their control of education.

In 1899 a Board of Education replaced the old Department, and became the sole central authority for primary, secondary and technical education. The struggles for local control was brought to a head by the Cockerton judgement. In this test case, a government auditor named James Cockerton, primed by a junior officer in the education department, took the London School Board to court. The court disallowed the Board's expenditure on science and art in higher grade schools because

> *such expenditure was not sanctioned under the 1870 and subsequent*

*Acts of Parliament. School Boards were competent to provide only
elementary education.*

This judgement prepared the way for the Balfour Act of 1902,
which gave to only 318 local authorities the responsibility which had
been distributed amongst 2,500 School Boards and 14,000 voluntary
school committees. The Act brought a few more local scholarships
but, even as late as the end of World War II, it was poverty that
prevented all but a trickle of children from attending grammar
schools. References to punishment ceased in the log books, because
schools were required to keep a separate punishment book. School
attendance became more strictly enforced.

Under the 1902 Act, School Board management committees were
replaced by committees responsible to the local authorities. But, for
Boughton Monchelsea School at least, the new management
committee was very similar in its composition to the old School
Board. Apart from the Vicar all were prominent landowners. Mr.
W. Braddick's father had made a fortune out of the West Indian slave
trade and, according to local legend, kept slaves in transit in a cellar
under his house at Boughton Mount.

In 1917, H.A.L. Fisher, historian and Minister of Education
claimed that:

*If anyone has doubted the value of our elementary schools, that doubt
must have been dispelled by the experience of the War.*

His 1918 Education Act abolished fees for elementary schools,
forbad the employment of children under 12 and controlled that of
children over 12, provided for sporting and recreational facilities in
schools, and gave the local education authorities power to raise the
leaving age to 15.

Fine work so far as it went – but even that was to be cut back
almost immediately by the 'Geddes Axe' of 1921. The National
Committee on Public Expenditure recommended that grants to
education be cut by a third, teachers' salaries be reduced and their
pension scheme put on a contributory basis. The 'Axe' led to absurd
economies in both buildings and staff and put back the course of
educational development for many years. Because, educationally,
Britain is still a divided nation, education cuts are in times of

difficulty amongst the first to be considered.

The reality of secondary education was that very few children indeed went to the grammar school, and this remained true until well after the Second World War. Few parents could afford to send their children even if they won a scholarship, because of the expense of uniform and travel and especially the surrender of the child's wage; and economics was reaffirmed by low expectations. I find only six names of children going on from Boughton to grammar school between 1907 and 1921 – one of them the headmaster's son.

It is true that, in compliance with the 1918 Act, all children sat for the ancestor of the 11 + rather than the headmaster recommending them for a grammar school, but this made slight difference in practice. Someone who sat this exam in 1924 said he never knew he was sitting it until long afterwards and that certainly neither he, nor his father, would have expected him to go on to higher education. The pattern of poverty and thwarted ability is clear:

And my sister-in-law, as soon as she got old enough to leave school she had to. Her mother said 'You're not going to no grammar school' and she tore up everything and she wouldn't hear anything about it. She had to go to work and she worked at what was then the Home and Colonial in Week Street, Maidstone.

(Dorothy Froud)

One of the Colegate boys who lived in the cottage by the Albion, he got through to the Grammar School but his parents couldn't afford it. The only ones I remember going were Harry Wood and one of the Pearson boys. The others didn't go, you see, because although you had the schooling, as soon as it came to fruiting time, you were gone for six weeks fruit-picking to help get the money for the winter. I was lucky in that I didn't have to go but I had to get up at five in the morning before school to pick fruit in the allotments opposite Cornwallis School.

(Nellie Pledger)

My father who had cataracts of the eyes had had to give up building work and go on the farm for fifteen shillings in summer and twelve shillings in winter. But by this time he was blind and my eldest brother had been kicked by a horse at work and was in hospital with

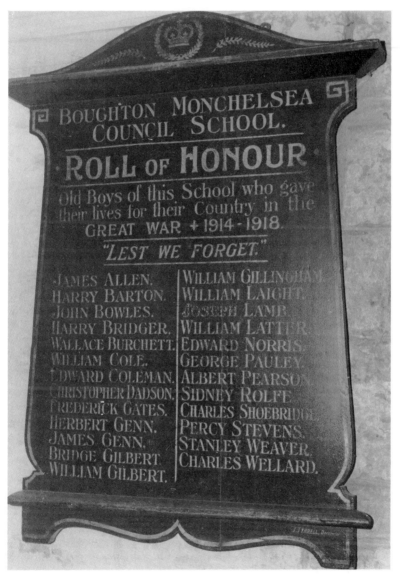

Roll of Honour Board. Great War 1914-18 made by boys of the school and still hung in the school.

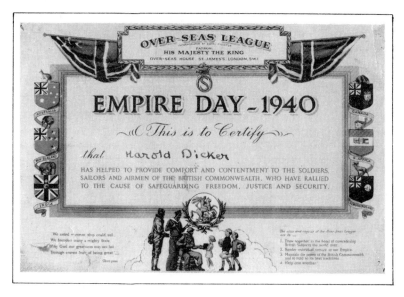

Overseas Club and League Certificates issued in the First and Second World Wars.

a diseased bone in the leg. So all the money coming in was a little bit of money from needlework, which my mother was doing. I was about 12 or 13 and there was a School Governor's meeting and I was allowed to leave. I was in X7 which was a pretty good going, though I don't want to boast about it. I got no prospects of ever getting beyond that school, probably because of the poverty in the family, which there was in dozens and dozens of other families.

(Tom Bridger)

-23-

The most pressing problem for Mr. P.R. Forder in his early years at the school was that of a rising school roll in the face of inadequate classrooms and staffing. The parish population, just over 1,000 hardly varied between 1872 and 1900, and, even by 1921, had only reached 1,269. The school roll, however, rose from 132 in 1872, to 240 in 1900. This is to be explained by the abolition of fees – the 'pence'[13] – and by stricter enforcement of attendance between 1890 and 1902, after which we hear less about offending landowners.

The frequent references to 'irregular attenders' both in the log books and the Board's or Committee's minute book is, of course, nothing new. But hitherto the importance of attendance was linked to the provisions of the Revised Code of 1862, which specified that grants to school should be dependent upon school attendance and annual examination in the 3 R's. After 1900, the drive for better school attendance was part of national policy to develop a more skilled workforce – a policy intensified by Britain's imperial ambitions now increasingly challenged by other industrial powers, notably Germany.

The Minute Book of the School Board is full of details about irregular attendance, and of warning notices being sent to parents or, in cases of total absence, to the employer.

Mr. Shadgett, the attendance officer, was very much feared. You only had to be away a couple of days and he'd be round to your home and if he thought you were all right, he'd order you back to school.

(Ron Costen)

[55]

Personal enforcement by the officer was backed by a willingness to prosecute parents and employers at the Bearsted Petty Sessions where, relative to the current agricultural wages of between 8 and 18 shillings a week, a fine of 6d. with 2 shillings costs may be counted as severe.

Two varieties of carrot were also tried. Half-day holidays were granted to the school by the managers for a high average attendance – in 1910, it was one half-holiday a month when the percentage attendance was at least 94 – and medals and certificates were awarded. They can still be seen framed on cottage walls. A medal signified that only a week had been lost from the year. In 1906, nearly a sixth of the school were awarded medals or certificates, so the inducement may have worked.

Of course there were the usual occasional absences due to local festivals, fairs and Guy Fawkes celebrations, though there is a marked decrease in such references. What are new are the many references to absence caused by 'beating' for one of the local landowners such as Mr. Cornwallis, Mr. Skinner or Mr. Kleinwort. By 'beating' was meant the employment of adults and children in order to raise the birds for a shoot. Whether such shooting was something new or whether it was hitherto felt not worth recording. I am uncertain. I have been told how Mr. Skinner or Mr. Cornwallis would simply walk into the school and demand, as of right, so many boys for beating.

> *Attendance low today. Many boys in Standard III and upwards, beating for Mr. Cornwallis.*

This is a common log entry. Examples of local events causing 'casual' absences include:

> *Many children absent today as the Yeomanry are operating in the neighbourhood.*

And schools are, of course, familiar with the attempt to associate the pleasures of a holiday with the institution of monarchy:

> *1897 School closed for two days in commemoration of her Majesty's Diamond Jubilee,*

1902 School closed for 6 weeks holiday, one extra week being granted for the King's Coronation.

1911 School closed until June 29th on account of the measles and the King's Coronation holiday.

1922 School closed with the express wish of H.M. the King – the Wedding of Princess Mary.

Less regular events included:

1900 Half-day's holiday given in honour of the Relief of Mafeking

1919 A day's holiday given to-day by order of the Committee in honour of the signing of the Peace Treaty.

As often as not, however, the 'holiday' meant another form of supervised activity:

1927 Half holiday for Maidstone Elementary School Sports

1937 School closed. The staff and 40 children attended the dress rehearsal of the Aldershot Tattoo

So it appears that attendance at school is a composite behaviour, made up from what looks like the child or family's decision, combined with the official ideas at any given time. This is clearest of all with children being 'allowed' to miss school in order to eke out the agricultural labour force.

During the fruiting and harvesting season boys of 12 and over could be claimed by their parents if they put in enough attendances during the year; to be set to work in the fields for six weeks. Proof had to be given that they did go to work.

Nellie Potter *(née Tree)*

The beginning of hop-picking or 'fruiting' still had a dramatic effect on attendance, even though the dates for the summer holiday were made flexible in order to meet the hop-harvest needs of any particular year. More drastically, children could legally be 'allowed' to attend half-time in order to work on the land. This requires some explanation.

Half-time for factory children had existed under the 1870

Education Act but, whereas they spent half the day in a factory and half the day in school, rural children would miss school for some months in the summer. The Agricultural Children's Act of 1875 attempted to deal with the widespread employment of children in agriculture but the Bill was weakly drafted and lacked any enforcing agency. In 1876 a second general Education Act was passed providing for attendance committees where no school board bye-laws operated.

Only in 1890 was an act passed which unequivocally imposed compulsory attendance on all children between the ages of 5 and 10 (raised to 11 in 1893).[14] Legal exemption for part-time attendance could still be obtained if the child had passed an examination at 11 and if a specified number of attendances had been made. Complete exemption below the age of 14 depended either upon the child gaining his 'Labour Certificate' at the standard laid down in the local bye-laws (usually standards IV or V); or upon having reached the age of 13 and having made at least 250 attendances per annum for the previous five years. This latter exemption was known as 'The Dunces Certificate'.

For 1897, however, we read:

Several of the children who have qualified for half-time are at (full-time) work in spite of the bye-laws published by the Board.

-24-

A major obstacle to attendance continued to be epidemic illness. References to this actually increase in the log, reflecting greater health consciousness;

1891 whooping cough
1892 mumps; caused poor attendance for 2 months
1893 whooping cough
1896 whooping cough and ring-worm
1900 scarlet fever
1904 scarlet fever
1908 scarlet fever and measles; school closed for a further
    fortnight by order of Dr. Tew, Medical Officer of Health

Boys gardening class with Mr Forder 1910.

Girls gardening class with Mr Fuller 1937.

Mr Fuller. Mr Plowright. Miss Longman. Miss Twigg. Mrs Thomas C1930.

Dorothy Beale and Minnie Wallis who
competed in District Sports Maidstone
Athletic ground 1938

1909 chicken pox
1911 whooping cough and measles
1912 scarlet fever, chicken pox and diptheria
1914 diphtheria
1915 diphtheria
1918 diphtheria, mumps and influenza. 'Staff and children
greatly affected'. (This was the world-wide influenza
epidemic which caused more deaths than the war itself.)
1919 chicken pox and diphtheria
1921 chicken pox
1922 whooping cough and measles

The litany could be continued into the next period:

1925 whooping cough, mumps and chicken pox
1927 influenza
1928 scarlet fever
1930 scarlet fever
1932 chicken pox
1933 whooping cough, diphtheria
1934 whooping cough, diphtheria
1943 chicken pox

Amongst the cuprits were, no doubt, the open cess-pits and the poor state of the outside lavatories which even in the 1950's used to be frozen for weeks in the winter, Certainly H.M. Inspectors made frequent references both to cess-pit and 'offices'.

After the Great War, a considerable advance was made in health and welfare provision. Apart from the introduction of school meals and (in 1946) free milk, a school medical service was established, which brought a new awareness of preventive medicine. We can trace the build-up. In 1900, we first hear of the 'Medical Officer', though the Sanitary Inspector is still mentioned in the same year. In 1911, the School Nurse makes her appearance:

Five children excluded for ten days on account of verminous state.

The Maidstone School Clinic followed in 1920, reference to a dental nurse in 1921, a visit by a dentist in 1922, and in 1923

Officer of the S.P.C.C. visited this morning and consulted the Master re condition of several children.

It is worth emphasising that there were no school meals or even satisfactory drinking water provided for the children. Mains water was not supplied until 1903.

> *There was, of course, no school milk, a drink of the water from the school well in an old chipped mug was all there was, and that, I, for one, was not allowed to drink. There was no canteen and children had to bring something to eat if they lived too far to go home for dinner.*
>
> **(Miss Wood,** *circa 1900)*

> *I will add, too, that lots of children were sent with no breakfast and quite often a child lost his dinner to a hungrier boy or girl.*
>
> **(Nellie Potter,** *circa 1906)*

In the context of the time, the Boughton Monchelsea and District Gospel Temperance Society should perhaps be counted amongst the welfare agencies. It was allowed to use the school for meetings, and to lecture the children on Temperance and 'The Hygiene of Food and Drink'. Visits from the Band of Hope continued into the second war.

> *Mr. Harvey he came every year, for years and years. You know, he put it over so badly, it didn't affect us at all. Afterwards I wondered what it was all about.*
>
> **Janet Stables***(née Bowles)*

> *This old man came to give us a talk on Health and Hygiene; he was a little man with a Van Dyck beard. And we'd all sit there and wait for him to write Food and Brink, not Food and Drink; it was always Food and Brink. That was what we all used to wait for, to see him write in beautiful copper plate on the blackboard.*
>
> **Pam Thresher***(née Button)*

And whilst we speak of Hygiene and Temperance, let us not forget their sister Thrift:

Penny Bank commenced today 1909.

Finally, amongst factors preventing attendance at school, especially for the poorer families, the weather should be given its due:

Children often came to school with shoes that barely covered their feet and, sometimes, even in winter, with no socks or stockings. There were no wellingtons for anyone as they were then quite unheard of and no mackintoshes. Therefore children on wet days often arrived at school really soaked to the skin and as roads then were very muddy, some covered in several inches of it, they were in pretty poor shape for learning.

Nellie Potter(*née Tree*)

Similar reports go on into the thirties. Still, when the thaw came after the severities of early 1927 (with coal in short supply since the General Strike), the willing children of the flooded Beult area

set out on their long journey on stilts leaving them at a certain point to be collected on their way home.

Greta Bowles (*née Harling*)

-25-

What was it like in the classrooms? Crowded, for a start. In 1889 the rooms and seats were listed: Large Room, 110; Class Room, 37; Infants Room 70, Total 217. A new classroom for 40 was added in 1906, the Inspector having commented that

The main room is overcrowded; there is no space for the First Standard who sit huddled in the corner, without desk accommodation, and cannot be well managed or taught, while they interfere with the other children.

In the reminiscences of even much later pupils, there is a streak of amazement that any teaching could have been achieved under the conditions. More than one class in the same room, facing different ways –

I can never understand how they managed, but then of course we were quiet. Talking was out.

Ena Greenaway(*née Potter*)

There were four classrooms and seven standards, plus infants. Miss Twigg and Mrs. Foster taught two infant classes and standard one, in the west room facing out to the south and the school yard. The lower windows swung inwards from the bottom and were of opaque glass. The next room, which was divided from the eastern – most classroom by a folding partition, was the top classroom. Here, Mr, Plowright took special lessons, and it was used for school medicals, when the windows were shrouded in white curtains and the partitions were covered with white drawing paper. There was another partition which divided it from the main hall, which I think was the original school. At school assembly in the mornings, one partition was slidded right back, and the door of the other partition was opened and the headmaster could conduct morning prayers for the whole school.

(Greta Bowles)

Then the classrooms were rather dim and often cold. There were hanging oil lamps – as late as 1923 it was considered too expensive to lay on gas to the school. The children took turns to be near the fire and the memories are all of cold. Many times I have been told how teachers used to block out the fire by standing with their backs to it .

The intensity of the weather to-day has made it impossible to keep the buildings satisfactorily warm. Several short breaks for physical exercise. (December 1927)

Only gradually, as stoves began to replace coal fires (1915), low ceilings were fitted and new classrooms were built (after World War II) was there any real improvement. In my own early years I remember ink freezing in the inkwells as children sat in their overcoats.

In 1893, the Inspector's Report observed that the classrooms were in need of 'apex ventilation' and goes on to comment on the overcrowded infant room where two or three classes 'are far removed from the fire'. The contradiction between apex ventilation and warmth was not apparent. The School Board's ensuing minute may stand for the methods of that day:

> *Read letter the Clerk addressed to the Education Department on 29th June last; the reply of the Department thereto, dated 17th July last; The Clerk's letter to the Department dated 27th July last; the Department's reply dated 1st August; the Clerk's further letter to the Department dated 4th instant and the Department's reply dated 12th instant.*
>
> **(School Board Minute, 1893)**

This correspondence dragged on for over a year before the Clerk reported that

> *the building work had been completed to the entire satisfaction of the Board. It was not found necessary to consult an architect.*

This work was carried out by Messrs. James Wood of Boughton Monchelsea. Indeed, it would appear that all the major building and decorating work of the school was carried out by Messrs. James Wood of Boughton Monchelsea. Besides giving much employment to local men, he kindly gave his time as a school manager. By coincidence, the school managers accepted all his tenders – even when his were not the lowest amongst the dozen or so local firms. For example, when in 1912 Wood quoted for 'summer repairs', and seven local firms made tenders ranging from £94 to £109, James Wood's tender was slightly above that of Walters Brothers'. The minute book reads:

> *Mr. Walters' tender was not in 'form' and the meeting recommended the K.E.C. to accept Mr. Wood's tender.*

More often, however, knowledge of the other tenders may have enabled Woods to undercut competitors.

The materials of a school include rubbers and black lead as well as the buildings. One could write an oblique history by setting down the

requisitions for educational and domestic supplies at different stages:
In October 1891

the Clerk to the School Board was directed to issue an order to the
following:
Edgar Britton – to supply drapery
Haynes Bros – ironmongery
G. Coleman – coal
The Educational Supply Association – stationery.

In 1892,

orders were issued for 25 bundles of faggots from T. Hubbard and a
wood chopper from Starnes of Maidstone.

In 1907 the following were ordered:

12 yards of house flannel
6 boxes of soap
6 boxes of black lead
1 hand broom and
6 Vestas lamp chimneys

As regards educational supplies

65 Geography Readers
12 dozen exercise books
2 boxes slate pencils
3 dozen Arithmetics.

(School Board Minute, July 1890)

The requisitions had to be sanctioned by the Board and later by the managers, the chairman countersigning the headmaster's order. In the early 1900's the school was more than once desperate for supplies:

Schools very short of pens, pencils, rubbers, etc. Work almost at a
standstill.

At such a stage, the school was still beholden to the local gentry for

Here My Caravan Has Rested. School concert 1933.

Sleeping Beauty. 1962. Ann Lamb centre middle row.

Class photos as a measure of change. 1901.

1928.

1949.

1962.

Mrs Watts takes her class on a Nature Walk 1955.

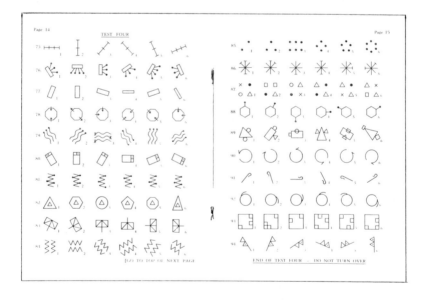

Kent Non Verbal Intelligence Test, part of the 11 + .

the charitable distributions of essay and gardening prizes, books and even tennis balls.

-26-

Memories of school in those days tend to be shaped by the contrast of kindly teachers to severe ones, and they are dominated by the issue of punishment. Moreover, we are dealing not directly with children's opinions but with reminiscence of childhood filtered through subsequent experience. Punishment will be seen in terms of the adult's estimate of current trends and their causes. No doubt, in more deferential times the harsh punishment was more acceptable, but in speaking of it now the older people commonly made comparisons with 'today's youth' and what is to be done about that. Most of those to whom I listened regarded the quite indiscriminated use of the cane – not just for naughtiness but as an 'educational' instrument – as completely justified, and point to today's 'indiscipline' as a result of its near-abolition. It would make no difference if I pointed out that today the local secondary school does not need a monitor to report **daily** on the window breakages in the school. My point here is not, however, to argue about corporal punishment but rather to caution that some of the oral evidence, which apparently gives us such direct and concrete access to the past, may in fact be tendentious. Again, it is a commonplace that images of 'the good old days' usually depend on selection and revision. Nor should we underestimate the artist in each informant, who tends to dramatise and shape a story out of the humdrum material of the past.

Nevertheless, old people must be largely accurate in remembering that they accepted their school experience in spite of conditions which today we should find degrading and intolerable. This is a reflection on the harshness of life for children outside school, when the alternative was hard physical labour from early morning until bedtime; and it was sustained by the social deference I have already tagged with the lines

> God made them, high and lowly
> And ordered their estate.

At the same time, a good deal of bitterness comes through in the reminiscing:

> *The junior master was very spiteful with the cane; he always had it handy for girls as well as boys.*
>
> **(Nellie Potter)**

> *Some teachers at this school used to hit you really hard across the back or across the knuckles, which I do not think helped the children to learn. You were punished for not understanding. At the woodwork centre at Loose, Mr. Reedside would fling lumps of wood at you if you were not attending. One day a group of us boys arrived late and he asked us how many miles we had walked. Then he gave us the number of strokes with the cane according to the miles we said we had walked.*
>
> **(Ron Costen)**

> *I forget the infant mistress's name, as they changed about, but I well remember her telling us wee mites that if we were naughty we would go to hell and burn for ever and ever and ever.*
>
> **(Miss Wood circa 1900)**

> *There were one or two I didn't like and that was because they used to cane you for no reason at all; that's what we used to think.*
>
> **(Ron Costen)**

> *Some of the teachers used to look down on the children – especially the poorer children; they used to have favourites you know. If anyone was better off, like the Bouldens or the Goodwins, that was different.*
>
> **(Dorothy Froud)**

-27-

In 1894, Elementary Science appears on the syllabus. Here is the programme for the following year:

Poetry for Repetition

Standard II   *Miller of the Dee*

	Minstrel Boy
Standard III	*After Blenheim – Southey*
Standard IV	*Armada – Macaulay*
Standards V, VI, VII	*Armada*
	Address to the Morning in Belzon's Exhibition – H. Smith

Needlework
Girls   *According to code*

Geography
Boys   *Standards I, II, III according to Code*
                                   Standards IV, V, VI VII –
                                   Europe Maps Spain & Portugal
                                   France
                                   The Rhine

History
Work to Standard IV – Twenty stories from Biographies 1485 – 1688

Elementary Science
Standard III   A selection of topics

1. *Water Liquid & solvents*
2. *Water – other forms*
3. *The Air*
4. *Nature of Gas*
5. *Gases of Liquids*
6. *Products of Coal*
7. *Dicotyledons*
8. *Monocetyledons*
9. *Manufacture of Linen*
10. *Classifications of the Animal Kingdom*

Object Lessons – Standard I *(a Selection)*
Cork and cork tree, oak tree, apple, orange, ship, railway station, coal and coal-pit, clock, silver, thimble

Object Lessons for Infants *(a Selection)*
china cup and saucer, lead pencil, iron and steel, copper, gold, silver, slate, glass, coal, iron, apple, orange, oak tree, wheat, horse,

elephant, camel, cow, fox and sheep.

Certain activities are not covered by such a list. While the girls were sewing (a machine was first suggested in 1913) and learning how to work and launder, the boys were doing carpentry and technical drawing. Such a division was obviously geared to their employment prospects. There was Biblical Instruction for all. Singing was prominent – in 1895, the following works were mastered:

> *Ye Sòft Blue Eyes*
> *A Merry Lad, the Farmer Boy*
> *O Happy is the Farmer's Life*
> *Drive the Nail Aright Boys.*

But the school's first piano did not come until 1926, only just before a gramophone.

In 1908, the Managers minute receipt of a pamphlet on Rural Education and by 1910 gardening was on the syllabus. In 1916, it was reported:

> *Lessons on the principal crops and pests with drawings in colour, supplements the outdoor work usefully.*

Girls and boys alike were

> *drilled army fashion with what were known as dumb-bells, which were pieces of rounded wood with blocks at each end.*
>
> **(Nellie Potter)**

The Boer War had revealed a low standard of physical fitness and from then on physical training was part of school life and assumed a military character.

> *It was resolved that the chairman should try and make arrangements for drill to be given to the children by a corporal from the Barracks at Maidstone at 2 shillings and 6 pence per week for 26 weeks. The Chairman was asked to see Mr. Cornwallis with a view to organising the matter.*
>
> **(Managers Minutes, June 1900)**

[74]

At the same time, the children wrote about 'The Expansion of the British Empire' (1900) and a prize essay was set on 'Causes which have promoted the advancement of Great Britain' (1902). These strands were to be woven together:

> *The Headmaster reported that the girls in the school had been knitting for the soldiers for the last month.*
>
> ***(Managers Minute**, Nov. 20th 1914)*

> *The Roll of Honour containing 25 names of the 'old boys' who lost their lives in the Great War was unveiled this morning by General Rodney Style. The board comprising the memorial was made by the boys at their handicrafts class and the decoration carried out by a Maidstone decorator; the cost being defrayed by a subscription from the children and staff.*

We have said that life would never be quite the same again: in particular, the landowners would not always be able to assume that children were simply a larval form of agricultural labour. But in 1914 it was still the case that

> *Most of the school governors was agricultural people and what they was after was somebody to do the work on the farm. So as soon as I got top of the class I wasn't worth anything to them – they just said 'Get on the farm' and that's what I had to do. My brother was called up off the farm when he was 18 and dead and buried before he was 19.*
>
> *(**Tom Bridger**)*

Chapter IV: 1923–1948

– 28 –

S o many 'improvements' took place between the wars – including a canteen (1925), gas (1933), and flush lavatories (1936) – that it would be easy to write up a miscellaneous record of achievement like a school magazine, complete with sports results and leaving presents. Less extreme poverty and better trained staff enabled such development. Its form, however, was decided by the tasks imposed at a particular time on a school in a particular kind of community.

> *The boys no longer mainly went to the farm but often became artisans or entered various trades. The girls mostly went into office work or shops; not many went into domestic service. The evening classes for typing and so on in Maidstone were very popular. They were something like a shilling an evening.*
>
> **(Janet Stables)**

We have seen that changing requirements for labour, relayed by national policy for education, not only altered the content of learning but also insisted that it make a more complex claim on the time and energy of the child. Direct knowledge of agriculture – 'learning from Jack' – no longer sufficed. The child must follow an organised curriculum which contained some of the same matter but in a more technically structured form. As late as 1938 we still hear of 'children absent on account of hop-picking' but already in 1923 the K.E.C. Horticultural Superintendent was reporting:

> *Plans of the cropping and garden are drawn to scale. A table showing the progress of the crops is kept. Notes are made of lessons given on insect pests, propagating and general vegetable culture. Arithmetic is also correlated.* **General Remarks:** *The scholars are keen gardeners and get good results.*

What happened between the wars was that the old order of the countryside was gradually superseded by a new discipline in which schooling was to play a key role.

– 29 –

The strongest contribution to this process at Boughton was made by John Plowright, who was headmaster from 1923 – 1936.

In my first term Mr. Plowright visited the school. I well remember the party of governers around the tall, dark man with shiny black hair and a small black moustache. After they had gone we were told that this was to be our new headmaster, and that he had been a soldier in India. Mr. and Mrs. Plowright were both trained musicians.

Greta Bowles)

He was a disciplinarian in such a charming manner. He was a tall man, good looking, with a small moustache. He walked very upright and I think he was upright in everything he did.

(Janet Stables)

He was popular, used to go about singing; he had a good tenor voice and she used to play for him. He had a great interest in sweet-pea growing – he used to pack them up and send them to Harrisons in Maidstone. He used to show his sweet-peas at all the great Agricultural Shows

(Mrs. Leeson, née Munn)

He used to play the piano and we, more or less, had community singing, and from this he drew his singers for his concerts at Christmas. He was very strict but wasn't unkind. I think most of the children had a great respect for him

(Pam Thresher)

Mr. Plowright was a dedicated man and man that was fair – fair almost to the point of sticking to the letter rather than to the spirit of something. He used to work too hard. He'd no sooner go in for his

[77]

dinner than he'd be out again doing the garden or something.
(Catherine Thrift, *Canteen Cook)*

In 1927, he was joined as assistant master by John Fuller who, unusually, was to go on to become the next headmaster (1936 – 1948). As H.M. Inspector reported:

> *He formerly served as an assistant and therefore has a knowledge of the difficulties resulting from the inconvenient nature of the school.*

He was a well-trained educator who was eventually to be awarded an M.B.E. for his services on the Newson Committee. Forceful and ambitious, he was to concentrate heavily on the brighter pupils and on building up the school's reputation

> *I must be fair but I think if you were on the bright side you went down alright but if you were struggling, and I was a bit of a struggler, and you wanted some individual attention, it wasn't given. I don't think it was entirely his fault for I think he had it in his mind that so-and-so is going to get a scholarship if he works a bit harder. I think he picked on the ones that were going and I knew I wasn't going.*
>
> **(Anon)**

> *I think he was very well liked and I've never heard anything against him. I liked him but then I liked school; it partly depended on how you did at school.*
>
> **(Peggy Latham** *née Dadson)*

> *He was liked by everyone and did an awful lot towards the good name Boughton had for sport.*
>
> **(Gertie Marsh)**

> *I think Mr. Fuller was quite feared as well as respected. I think he was a good teacher*
>
> **(Vera Davis)**

The quality of other staff was now much improved. One, Margaret Longman, who served for 33 years, epitomised the best teaching and also lets us glimpse a common form of loss and displace-placement in the 1920's:

[78]

She was a nice person; her young man was killed in the First War. She treated us ever so well; everyone liked her. She was there for years.

(Dorothy Froud)

In fact, her fiancé had been killed with a hundred others in an explosion at a munitions factory in Faversham.

She was very patient, very good with the slow learners and marvellous with Grace Kimber, who was deaf and dumb. Today she would have been a good special school teacher

(Nigel Fenner)

(Grace was later sent to a special school where nowadays she would have gone from the first.)

Miss Longman lost her boy-friend in the Faversham explosion. I remember hearing that explosion because I was in Mr. Forder's class at the time and he said it was a ladder being moved on the roof. I always remember him camouflaging that one. And I remember that was a great set-back for Miss Longman, well, she never got likely to be married afterwards.

(Tom Bridger)

Miss Longman was very strict and straight-laced, very keen on posture. Many a time during sewing lessons she would slap me on the back and remind me 'if you crouch down like that you'll grow up pigeon-chested'.

(Gertie Marsh)

I remember her with her nut-wand. She used to give you a stroke with her nut-wand and stand you on a chair with your hands behind your head. But I still liked her.

She was very nice but a strickler for getting needlework just right — or else it would have to be undone and re-sewn.

(Janet Stables)

Miss Longman was appointed in 1911 and retired in 1944. She

kept in close touch with the village after retirement and sent a donation when the school swimming pool was built. She died in 1972.

Another such teacher was Miss 'Flossie' Twigg:

Miss Twigg was old-fashioned but she was very nice. She was a very good teacher; I know she wasn't certificated but an Act of Parliament came out that made all uncertificated teachers qualified; good teaching does not always depend on certificates.

Mrs. Catherine Thrift)

I can remember her sitting in that classroom as clear as day, because she was a lovely person. I can remember her now winning the confidence of that class because everybody liked her.

The kids used to run behind her up the village street. She had one of the old-fashioned bicycles – there weren't many cars were there? She was a lovely person and a dedicated teacher.

(Nigel Fenner)

Miss Twigg joined the staff in 1919 and retired in 1954. When she died a few years ago she left to me a large envelope of school photographs and other mementos. She was that sort of person.

-30-

Because of the war, the school roll dropped to 176 in 1929; but attendance was becoming more regular and the children were more attentive.

Not many were absent at harvest time though, if the hop-picking hadn't finished, children might be a week late coming back. I remember the Thirkells – two or three boys and Joan Thirkell – and they lived a long way from the bottom of Church Hill. They used to walk to school every day there and back and they were never late and never missed a day.

(Janet Bowles)

The improvement in attendance and discipline has been explained to me as due to improvement in the standard of living; and poverty certainly was less severe, although

> *In those days they didn't have socks and in cold weather like this they didn't have any warm clothes – I can remember Mr. Plowright asking us if we had any discarded clothes would we bring them up. There were children with hardly any soles, no socks and snow on the ground.*
>
> ***(Pam Thresher)***

Families would have been frightened, and grateful not to be worse off in England at that time:

> *We were often visited by what we called 'tramps' from the industrial midlands and north, seeking work. We had collections of clothing and produce at school and these were sent to 'black country' schools. From the families of some of these wandering unemployed we often had short-stay pupils at school. The plight of some of these children was disturbing... Many of them stayed in 'the Huts' after the hop-picking had finished. They often stood in pathetic groups in the playground and hardly dared to raise their voices above a whisper.*
>
> ***(Greta Bowles)***

Perhaps we can say that some economic improvement, combined with decreased need for child labour on the land, were sufficient for the school now to be considered less of a threat to family income.

A further reason for improved behaviour and better attendance must surely have been a changed curriculum; and particularly the emphasis placed on Games and Gardening, which were not only subjects of immediate interest to many children but also efficient channellers of energy. For a quarter of a century, the log book was to be dominated by references to the school garden and to athletics.

> *As a rural school we were encouraged to follow country pursuits.*
> ***(Greta Bowles)***

> *We could spend a lot of time on that gardening when I think back –*

[81]

weeded all that front garden, did the mowing, pruning the roses and weeding. I always liked it because it was a way of getting out of your maths or something like that. When something special was on, it was all hands to the pump, spruce right up you know. We spent a lot of time out there. It put the school on the map and athletics did that as well.

(Tom Bridger)

The 'something special' might be a distinguished visitor:

At 3 p.m. this afternoon, the Lady Colet Shield for gardening was presented to the school. Before and after the ceremony, the seniors sang songs and Mr. Smart was complimented on their excellent tone. The Rt. Hon. Lord Northbourne made the presentation and was accompanied by the Director of Education, the Agricultural Organiser and the Horticultural Officer. . . Lord Cornwallis and Mrs. Bluett Winch were also present.   *(1934)*

Mr. K. Lindsay, the Parliament Secretary to the Board of Education, visited the school.   *(1938)*

The school exhibited at the County Agricultural Show and classes were taken on carefully conducted tours of the orchards where a few years previously they might have played truant to go scrumping:

HMI having been notified, the boys of the gardening class spent the afternoon watching a demonstration of fruit tree pruning by Mr. W. H. Skinner on his land near the church.

'School journeys' were also paid to the gardens of Wierton Place, to a dairy and to a poultry farm; whilst the Head was permitted to attend the Chelsea Flower Show.

Nobody could say that Boughton Monchelsea children lacked cultivation:

The front garden was made ornamental. When the war came I persuaded Mr. Waters to let me have a bit of his plum orchard. He also let me run poultry underneath the plum trees and the droppings saved the trees. After the war the garden was planned in 4 house

[82]

plots, a fruit garden and twin annual borders, which could be seen from the infant door going south.

(Letter from John Fuller, 1979)

Part of the front garden has been turfed, to become a rose garden to commemorate the Coronation,

(Log, March 1937)

The 'correlation' with other subjects noted by the Horticultural Superintendent in 1923 could also be seen as annexation:

Garden frame made by boys at the Handicraft class from obsolete desks set up in school garden.

The Inspectorate did not perceive all this as 'a way of getting out of your maths':

Gardening is a particularly good feature of the work; flower and vegetable culture are being successfully undertaken. (1933)

The school is outstanding for its development of rural activities and the considerable part they play in the class-work of the older children. The result is a lively interest and sound practical approach to their lessons. (1947)

A school's reputation being founded on examination success, or distinction in this or that subject, is nothing new and must always raise doubts as to whether that reputation has been gained at the expense of a minority or even the majority of the other pupils. It is enough to point out that until 1936, the gardening was for boys only.

In addition to the usual exhibition of boys' vegetables and woodwork the girls this year exhibited needlework at Linton Flower Show. (1924)

Of course this exactly reflected what remained of the traditional occupations for men and women. At the time. however, the only serious and persistent criticism was anonymous:

The correspondent was directed to write to Mr. Peach asking him to destroy the rabbits in the school wood, as they were doing so much damage in the school gardens.

(Managers Minute)

Even now, the rabbits nest in the rose beds and disport themselves on the field during school hours.

-31-

The Inspector for 1933 also noted that 'the school has a praiseworthy record in connection with school athletics', and this is, indeed, the major innovation to the syllabus in the whole period.[15]

Mr. Fuller and Mr. Plowright asked any who lived near enough to return after school with any cutting instrument we could muster to cut the grass as short as possible, envisaging a week's work with a hundred keen children, plus any parents willing and able to help. In a week we had our race-track.

(Greta Bowles)

And for 3 or 4 years, for the size of the school, it pretty well ran away with the local sports. I've got all the photos of the athletic teams. We had a good football side, too.

(Dick Harris)

Nothing is more tedious than other people's sports results, but the reader may be assured that they were the marvel of the County.

Very early on a member of staff composed a school song for us, plus a cheer-ditty, which we would roar from our coaches as we passed the Cannon in Maidstone on our way to and from the athletic ground in London Road.

(Greta Bowles)

The importance of John Fuller in this mobilisation is clear:

The headmaster reported that Mr. Fuller had, during the holidays,

Linton Park CC winners of Village Championship at Lords 1978. Six ex-Boughton pupils, T 3,5,6. A. Piper, P. Bowles. T. Thirkell. B 2,4,5. J. Harris, N. Thirkell. P. Brattle.

A Pageant of Kent. 1965.

George Brooker.

Reg Copper.

attended a physical training course and was the only one, out of 300, who passed with credit.

(Managers Minute)

As before the First World War, the cult of physical fitness was associated with nationalism:

Half-holiday for the visit of H.R.H. the Prince of Wales to the County Fair. Forty children of this school took part in the Rally of Youth.

(Log, 1943)

The Rally of Youth had close links with such movements as the Keep Fit Movement, the Scout and Guide Movements and the Duke of York's Camps for Boys. The use of the word 'massed' in 1936 is disquieting:

To-day Saturday, the children gave a demonstration of Country Dancing, Maypole Dancing, Games, Gymnastics and Massed Physical Exercises.

Empire Day was always observed, and not only with essay prizes:

The flag-pole stood in the middle of the black iron railings that divided the school garden plots from the school yard. On St. George's Day and Empire Day it was used ceremoniously, when the whole school assembled in the yard, marched past and saluted the flag, and sang patriotic songs and hymns.

(Greta Bowles)

When John Fuller became headmaster in 1936, he announced the unity of these themes:

This week Classes, I, II, III have been arranged in four Houses: Canada, Australia, India and Africa. Eight house captains, four boys and four girls, have been chosen as well as a Head Boy and a Head Girl. The school has taken for its motto 'Play Up and Play the Game'.

[87]

The building of a canteen can be taken to mark the new insistence on welfare.

> *Mr. Galbraith, Medical Officer of Health, expressed himself delighted with the menus served and the cleanliness of the kitchen.*
>
> ***(Log, May 1925)***

Cooking was on a coal range and when gas finally came, it did so with a bang.

> *Upon the cook lighting the oven of the gas stove in the canteen kitchen, an explosion occurred. The front of the stove was wrecked but Mrs. Thrift, though badly bruised on the arm, was otherwise unhurt.*

The dinners were served in the large school room (now the hall):

> *We had about six or seven dinner monitors; three were servers, which meant we had to dish up the meals; the other three used to wait on the others. We had aprons and caps for the servers, the waiters carrying all the plates. We went to the canteen to collect the sweet whilst the waiters cleared the first course plates. After the others had finished, the waiters and servers were allowed to have theirs. Then we had the job of clearing up ready for afternoon lessons, so if you were a monitor that week you didn't have any time to play, but I don't recollect anyone saying they didn't want to do it; I don't think it ever occurred to us.*
>
> ***(Pam Thresher,** nee Button)*

The children near home didn't stay to school dinner, since most mothers didn't go to work and also many grew their own vegetables. Food was comparatively cheap and is one reason why the standard of living was even as high as it was.

Mrs. Catherine Thrift, the first school cook, speaks vividly about those days, and gives us an unusual viewpoint on the relationships of school life:

I came to Kent because my husband was a Kentish man; he was a fruitgrower and owned land locally.

I came to the job because I knew May Munn and she happened to mention me to Mr. Plowright.

Before I married I had been on very good service starting work at 14. I was about 27 or 28 when he asked me and it seemed a bit of a challenge.

There was a coal-fired kitchen range and an iron boiler for heating the water in the corner. There was a pipe chimney, no proper chimney, and believe me, the place was really cold.

I would give the order to Mr. Plowright and he gave it to one of the three shops in the village, a month for each in turn. On Fridays, he sent me down to pay the bills and my wages had to come out of the money collected for dinners, which at that time were two and half pence each.

I had to start getting the dinners ready at half-past eight. I didn't serve the food; the older children were given the job of taking the food in, serving it and having their own dinners afterwards. There were no accidents and very little breakages. Giving children responsibility makes them responsible.

The biggest job was cooking on a coal fire and I had to carry my own coal. Sometimes I had as many as 100 dinners to cook, but usually it was 70-80 a day. The older girls, when it was wet, would come in and give me a hand.

The boys had garden plots and we'd pay for vegetables into the Garden Fund, and I used to ask Mr. Plowright to order 5 cwt of potatoes at a time (we used to get a sack for about 5 shillings a hundredweight), a 112 lb sack of flour which I used to put in a new dustbin. I had no fridge of course, and little cupboard space and so I couldn't keep anything from one day to the next; everything had to be used up.

To Gas – with a Bang!

There wasn't much variety to the food because I only had so much money. But I cooked plenty of good solid food and fruit when we could get it. We were lucky in Kent, there was so much fruit around and since so many of the mothers went out to work I got fruit easily. Meat would come in fresh every morning. Once a week the children would have a really good soup with bones from the butcher and vegetables.

The farmers were good to me, so that sometimes I would find a sack of cauliflowers outside – the ones not good enough for market. I bought in bulk when I could.

The gas did make things a bit easier for me, though I wasn't pleased when I found this ugly great thing when I came back from my holidays; it had a big oven that opened outwards. With the condensation everything got rusty and I had to keep the windows open. I had to light it with a match. One day I thought I had lit it but the gas stopped half-way along and when I looked in the oven later on it had gone out. I struck a match again and the explosion threw me across the kitchen.

The canteen was built by voluntary contributions. Every Christmas we had a Christmas party. We had roast beef and Yorkshire pudding with trimmings. I'd go in on the Saturday morning to cook the Christmas pudding. I never got a penny piece for it but I enjoyed doing it. Mr. Plowright and I got on very well and nobody worried me.

I never got paid for the holidays, so I never made a fortune out of it, though I was there for 12 years. And I got the princely sum of twelve shillings and six pence a week.

When the canteen was taken over by the K.E.C., Mrs. Thrift resigned as she refused to accept reduced wages on account of the fewer school dinners being served.

Owing to a reduction in dinners it is necessary to reduce the cook's wages. Mrs. Thrift will not accept new terms. [16]

[90]

There were fewer dinners because with John Fuller's headship in 1936, the school lost its older pupils and became a junior mixed and infant school, leaving a roll of 109. Something of the kind had been envisaged as early as 1919[17] but the change now was propelled, like that in more than a thousand other schools, by the thinking of R.H. Tawney's **Secondary Education for All** (1922), followed up by the Hadow Committee whose Report was endorsed by the Board of Education. This line of thinking reconsidered the whole purpose of educational knowledge:

> *The schools whose first intention was to teach children how to read have. . . been compelled to broaden their aims until it might be said now they have to teach children how to live.*
> *(Hadow Committee, **The Primary School**, 1933)*

In particular, the adolescent needed an appropriate schooling that was hard to provide in a school that also catered for infants. In view of these and economic considerations – not least the high rate of juvenile unemployment – a secondary school system was recommended. The first Hadow Report called for experiment in multi-bias (that is, 'comprehensive') schools but in general proposed grammar schools with maximum opportunity for entry.

The Federation of British Industries, which earlier had opposed the Fisher Education Act on the grounds that

> *Industry would be unable to bear the burden of releasing its juvenile labour*

now claimed that

> *only a small minority of children were mentally capable of benefiting from secondary education.*

It is less understandable that a former medical officer could write in 1928:

> *most elementary children cannot benefit from secondary education*

[91]

because of the shallowness of their mental process.

This kind of thinking owed much to a school of psychology which laid great stress on the hereditary factor and claimed that intelligence was measurable and unalterable, so that the authorities could sort children at the age of 11 into fitting schools. The Spens Committee (1938) – impressed by the evidence of Cyril Burt which has since been proved highly questionable and, in part, fraudulent – was to proclaim that

> *with very few exceptions, it is possible at a very early age to predict the ultimate level of children's intellectual powers.*

It was confidence in this predictability that promoted the emerging pattern of dividing secondary education into grammar, technical, and modern schools.

The immediate consequence for the new primary school was, of course, the anxiety of the scholarship exam.

> *Everybody sat the Scholarship Examination. Most of them didn't stand a chance. The boys and girls grammar schools each had only a two form entry, about 60 children for each, and half of these places would be for fee-payers.*
>
> **(Dick Harris)**

> *I took the grammar school exam at 11 and I was terrified. I remember going up to the grammar school and sitting in isolation in the hall; you had to go there to sit part one. I took one look at the school and I didn't want to go there and I didn't even try.*
>
> **(Vera Davis)**

> *It was so different in my day, no open evenings and nobody ever explained anything to parents.*

> *I had this form to be taken home to my grandfather for him to sign and give me permission to sit the scholarship examination. I never gave it to him because, being a bit on the bright side, I really didn't want to leave the school and my friends. I would have walked it, I think, but I thought I'll stay put. Because with a lot of my friends,*

their parents couldn't afford to let them go because of the cost of the uniform. You must remember in my day you didn't go into Maidstone; it was quite a treat. Today, it would have been followed up – and that's an advantage of a school being open. I've bitterly regretted not going ever since.

(Pam Thresher)

Accordingly, between 1923 and 1936 the school 'sent' less than a dozen pupils to grammar and technical schools. Two successes in 1925 warranted a half-holiday.

For the purposes of this brief history, it should also be pointed out that the change from an all-age to a primary school affects the quality of oral evidence. Those who left at 11 are unlikely to retain such vivid impressions as those who left at 14 and before 1936.

> *It must be remembered that this was not a primary school but a school where a child spent the whole of his school life and at 14 was often jolly glad to leave.*
>
> *(Nellie Potter)*

-34-

Mr. Rush was half way through his sermon and Mr. Pledger walked up the aisle just to say we'd declared war and Mr. Rush burst into tears.

(Harold Dicker. then 9 years old)

750,000 CHILDREN TO BE EVACUATED IN ENGLAND AND WALES – September 1st, 1939.

> *There were three times as many of them as there were village children; a hell of a lot and they seemed to be everywhere. I remember them coming, there were coach loads of them down by the Rec. You must remember this was a little village school and they came and they swamped it. We didn't get on well with the London children, we split up into separate schools; we just couldn't mix. The majority were a real rough and tumble lot; they could pick a fight. They were*

[93]

totally different; remember it was a country life here then
(*May Dicker* née *Millin*)

The four we had at Elm House were all under nine and couldn't be placed elsewhere. We turned all the furniture out of the drawing room and put up camp beds with straw palliasses; they made a tremendous mess of that front room.

They had very little in the way of clothes, hardly any, so our mother had to go out and buy some. They were very much 'alive' and so we had to treat their heads with fig oil and cut off their hair.

Our aunts at Lyewood had two or three boys and one day the aunts went into their bedroom and found them sleeping not on the bed but under the bed because in their part of the world with families having so many in one room, that's what they did.
(*Barbara and Rachel Smith*)

BRITISH ARMY EVACUATED FROM DUNKIRK – May 27th-4th June, 1940

I remember coming out of church on a beautiful September Sunday morning and the sky was alive with dozens of 'dog-fights' overhead. It was the day we shot down 126 enemy aircraft.
(*Rachel Smith*)

The thing that was most frightening was when we had the Battle of Britain. But I don't think we realised it at the time because we all stood outside looking up at it. We had gas masks in their cases and when we went to the shelter we had to file out of the classrooms and put on our gas masks. I'm claustrophobic and there was no air in there. We were often only in there minutes, but it seemed like hours.
(*Nigel Fenner*)

In spite of the sound of bombs dropping, morale of the children excellent.
(*Log*, *August 15th, 1940*)

He sat and talked about the aeroplanes when the Battle of Britain

Fathers digging foundations of swimming pool Easter 1969.

The completed pool building 1971.

Adventure Playground 1969 showing tower, bridge and amphitheatre.

Adventure Playground showing maze, sand pit and school woods.

was on and said how, one day, we were all going up in aeroplanes.

During the weekend all First Aid equipment of the Maidstone Rural District and all protection given to the First Aid Post removed from the School. The main room now has no protection against glass splinters, the other windows of the school having been protected with adhesive strips by the teachers at their own expense. As it is not considered necessary to take these precautions in rural areas, the Committee are unable to supply the adhesive paper for the purpose.

(Log, *August 5th, 1940)*

In spite of letters from the Head Teacher, Managers and Parents, the K.E.C. has done nothing yet to the school to afford protection against air-raids. During air-raids this week the fall of bombs and the rattle of machine guns could be heard distinctly. Many enemy aircraft have passed over the school.

(Log, *August 16th, 1940)*

A letter was received from the K.E.C. stating that they did not recommend anything being done for A.R.P. and that the children should remain in school in the event of an air-raid warning.

(Managers Minute, *1940)*

The covering of all windows with wire netting commenced.

(Log, *August 19th, 1940)*

The Parents met the Managers this evening at 6.30 to discuss the protection of children in air-raids. A petition was drawn up and signed by all the parents that the K.E.C. should provide an air-raid shelter.

(Log, *August 20th, 1940)*

Air-raid shelters commenced.

(Log, *February 1941)*

The planes used to go over in their hundreds in the Battle of Britain and we used to lie on that old water tank and count them, and chalk up a hundred bombers. And then fighters and more fighters came up from the Weald; we used to get right excited.

(May Dicker)

BATTLE OF BRITAIN ENDS – September 15th 1940
AEROPLANES LOST: LUFTWAFFE, 1,733. R.A.F. 915.

To reduce as much as possible the risk of congregating pupils in one place, half the children – those who live at a distance to attend in the morning and the others in the afternoon. Many children were not sent because no air-raid shelter. Owing to air-raid warning, afternoon school could not commence until 2.45 p.m.
Children marked and then attendance cancelled to fulful regulations of the code.

(Log, *October 7th, 1940)*

Mr. A.B. Jones ceased duty at this school to-day to join the Army. Staff and children presented Mr. Jones with a fountain pen.

(Log, *February 1941)*

CLOTHES RATIONING COMMENCES – June 2nd, 1940

Mrs. Bracher, WVS, called to discuss the opening of a clothing exchange at school.

(Log, *February 1945)*

Dr. Taylor carried out a second diphtheria innoculation.

(Log, *September 1941)*

During the holidays, milk was distributed daily – all members of staff took turns in helping with the distribution.

(Log, *September 1942)*

I remember Mr. Fuller took over the allotments in Haste Hill and he used to march us along there – and the girls too where Goodwin's Chicken Farm used to be. I think it was all part of Mr. Fuller's Dig for Victory Campaign and the need to have extra produce for the canteen.

(Harold Dicker)

From today the keeping of poultry will form a part of the practical training of the older children. Mrs, Joan Clark has presented the school with light Sussex pullets. The house will be bought from the Garden Fund.

(Log, January 1941)

Mr. Gaynor (Plant Protection Company) gave a demonstration to the top class on the application of fertilizers and pest control – 'Grow More Food Compaign'.

(Log, May 1941)

Two chickens stolen during Friday night,

(Log, November 1941)

POINTS RATIONING SCHEME FOR BRITAIN – December 1st, 1941

Permission received from the K.E.C. to rent an additional 20 rods of orchard land, adjacent to the school garden – the four parish allotments being given up.

(Log, November 1944)

Between ten and fourteen I spent more time catching rabbits for Waters the Butchers than I did in school.

(Harold Dicker)

Head Teacher absent owing to strained abdominal muscle moving school chicken-house

(Log, May 1944)

JAPANESE ATTACK PEARL HARBOUR – December 6th, 1941

Special lessons to-day to mark American Thanksgiving Day.
(Log, November 26th, 1942)

We missed a lot of schooling, only going half-days. To be honest with you it was often not even that. A siren might go on the way to school – we could take shelter in a house, go on to school or go back home. Kids are going to go home, aren't they?

(Harold Dicker)

Owing to prolonged air-raid warning no afternoon children came to school.

(Log, *October 25th, 1940)*

Parents urged by letter to allow children to stay to dinner – 66 children had canteen dinner to-day.

(Log, *November 6th, 1940)*

SOAP RATIONED – February 9th, 1942

I remember we knitted for the forces. Miss Longman bought khaki, light blue and dark blue wool in bulk and we had a choice of knitting scarves, mittens and balaclavas in any one of these colours.

(Peggy Latham. *née Dadson)*

Empire Day Service held. A collection was made for the Comforts Fund – 16 shillings.

(Log, *May 1941)*

At 11.45 the school assembled to present Mrs. B. B. Jolly (Red Cross) with the money received for the collection of 14 cwt of waste paper and 15 shillings from an afternoon concert. The money received was sent to the Prisoner of War Fund.

(Log, *December 1942)*

The whole school assembled at 2.45 for a concert, each class providing a number of items. A collection was made which realized nine shillings towards the cost of the school wireless licence.

(Log, *April 1943)*

Whole school assembled at 11 a.m. for Schools Empire Broadcast. £1 was collected for Empire Overseas Tobacco Fund.

(Log, *May 1943)*

School Wings for Victory Week commenced.

(Log, *June 15th, 1943)*

Miss Smith visited school in the morning to judge Wings for Victory posters and models.

(Log, June 17th, 1943)

Whole school assembled at 2.45 to hear a talk given by Flying Officer Skipper.

(Log, June 1943)

Mr. Harvey gave a lecture today, Class I, on the Hygiene of Food and Drink.

(Log, 1944)

EUROPE INVADED BY 4,000 SHIPS: D-DAY – June 6th, 1944

Prior to D.Day, Monty was stationed at Boughton Mount and could be seen most mornings leading the troops on a morning run.

(Peter Barker)

Mrs. Kerr, WVS, visited with wellingtons for the older children. Donations to the Red Cross were made for the wellingtons.

(Log, March 1945)

FIRST V-1 FALLS ON ENGLAND – June 12th, 1944

During the doodle-bug period the Observer Corps had a base on Goodwin's Chicken Farm and on the approach of the doodle-bug a flare was fired into the air attached to a small parachute. This was done all along the route and enabled the aircraft to intercept more quickly. At one period the doodle-bugs passed over at 2 minutes intervals.

(Peter Barker)

Attendance poor owing to attack of pilotless planes. School closed in the afternoon for three weeks fruit-picking holiday.

(Log, June 1944)

I think we enjoyed the interruptions to normal routine. I was lucky in that living so near the school I was allowed home. When the engine stopped of a doodle-bug (VI rocket) we dived from our bikes under a bank. As soon as it was over we used to go off to see where it had come down.

(Margaret Woodhams née Barton**)**

Notice of Evacuation was received 7.30 p.m.
(Log, August 21st 1944**)**

A meeting of parents was held in the Village Hall at 7.30 p.m. when the Head Teacher spoke on evacuation and answered questions. At this meeting, Miss Longman, who is retiring this term, was presented with a cheque for £30 and an album containing the names of managers, staff past and present, scholars and friends who had subscribed to the testimonial.

(Log, August 22nd, 1944**)**

Ten children evacuated to-day to Aberayron, Wales.
(Log, August 27th 1944**)**

During the week war damage repairs were carried out to school and house.
(Log, November 1944**)**

This week a waste-paper and book drive was held. £1.7.0 handed over to Earl Haig's Fund.
(Log, November 24th, 1944**)**

Sub. Lieutenaut R. Anscombe, Fleet Air Arm visited the School. Classes 1 and 2 were assembled and the children asked questions on the R.A.F., the Fleet Air Arm and Training in America.
(Log, February 1945**)**

END OF WAR AGAINST GERMANY DECLARED – May, 8th, 1945

School closed for two days. V.E. holidays marking the end of the war in Europe. On May 9th the whole school went in procession to church to take part in a Thanksgiving Service.
(Log, May 8/9th, 1945**)**

Many children absent and, those present, very tired owing to previous day's festivities.

(Log, May 10th, 1945)

LABOUR VICTORY AT GENERAL ELECTION – July 26th, 1945

The Managers agreed that they would keep the air-raid shelters as a store and would like to have two doors fitted as entrances.

(Log, July 1945)

ATOMIC BOMB DROPPED ON HIROSHIMA – August 6th, 1945
JAPAN SURRENDERS UNCONDITIONALLY – August 14th, 1945

School closed for two days. V.J. (Victory over Japan) holidays, marking the end of the Japanese war. The whole school went in procession to church for a Thanksgiving Service.

(Log, August 15th, 1945)

Thanksgiving Savings Weeks commenced. Target £100.

(Log, October 1945)

Several children took part in the concert given in the Village Hall in aid of the Welcome Home Fund.

(Log, February 1946)

-35-

The school records show more about the second than the First World War, and the reasons are not hard to find. Troops were billeted in the grounds of Boughton Place, Wierton Place and Linton Park, with a Fire Training School in Linton Park; Kent was in the front line particularly during the Battle of Britain, at the time of the Normandy landing and during the V bomb attacks; and, because of wireless and a greater release of information, people were far more aware of what was happening.

And to each War, its Education Act. The McNair Committee reported in 1944 that

the nation as a whole has woken up to the deficiencies of its public educational system... we are witnessing one of the most widespread and insistent of popular demands for its reform.

The Butler Act passed in that year divided the system into primary, secondary and further education. Local authorities were required to provide free secondary education and the school leaving age was to rise to 15 and then 16. They were also to provide school meals and free milk, regular medical inspection and special education for the handicapped. It was now to be compulsory for schools to conduct, and children to attend religious instruction and a daily act of worship.

For a while, at least, Boughton Monchelsea School went on much as it had before the disruption of war. In the development plan for the County, it was earmarked for closure in favour of a new school in a nearby village. The managers, however, minuted this news at the same meeting as they made building plans for a canteen, confident in their argument that

The infants from 5 to 7 should remain in their own village.
(Managers Minute)

Even though all the grammar school places were now free, those going on to them from Boughton actually declined for a few years. [18] Prospects were still much the same as before the war:

One day we were asked all around the school what sort of jobs we hoped to be able to do when we left. I was far too young to have much idea. Very few girls said they would be going into service. I said my mother would not allow me to. Later I said I would like to work in a drapers shop because I liked fabrics, or in a library, or be an artist. We had no art classes. I was told these jobs were for ex-grammar school pupils only. Among the boys, three were going to follow their fathers on to the land. One of those intended to be a gardener.
(Greta Bowles)

If we contrive to finish our Chapter on a cheerful note', that is only the way innumerable Chirstmas terms ended.

The 'Waxworks' was a sketch at one of the concerts, when famous people were impersonated. My brother did 'Charlie Chaplin' and I think 'Harold Lloyd' was another. A double act with a pair of twin brothers, the 'Flea', a monologue, a shadow play, the first three act play, with sailors, a shipwreck, cannibals, and a rescue in the last act. This was the time when we were dressed in uniforms with beards that would not stay put, and my intended gruff seaman's voice came out as an embarrassed squeaky whisper. The captive sailors, bound, and awaiting their fate in the cannibals stew-pot, were regaled with a singularly sweet rendering of 'Who's dat a-calling' by a Linton Church solo choir-boy. How we enjoyed it all! Dancing a minuet in white wigs and pale blue knee-breeches suits, and partners in pastel crepe paper crinolines. A tambourine dance to a Swiss yodelling tune, with the stage bouncing up to meet our feet every time we moved.

(Greta Bowles)

At Christmas, Mr. Plowright always got up a party to sing for the Waifs and Strays and he used to take us and there'd be a whole gang of us.

Mr. Plowright would notify all the big houses as to which time it would be convenient to go. And each house in turn would have its own dinner party. Of course, Mrs. Foster Clark lived at Boughton Mount then. And we started off and we'd do all the big houses around.

Old Phil Bowles used to come with his fiddle and we had long poles with lanterns on them. And it always seemed to snow at Christmas and the moon used to shine and it was frosty and glittering. Wherever we went we were taken into the big houses. At Foster Clark's the grand piano was wheeled into the Conservatory and there were all the beautiful plants. There would be a dinner party of 20 or 30 people, and the choir would go in and sing. And often they gave us hot cocoa, an apple, an orange and a bag of sweets, brought up by the head parlour maid and the butler, and a big currant bun if we wanted one. And the grown ups – they'd always have drinks, and old Phil Bowles and Mr. Plowright would be almost reeling by the time we'd been all the way round – Beresfords, Lyewood, Wierton Place, Wierton Grange, Elm House, Boughton Place. We might collect £45 on one night for the Waifs and Strays.

(Pam Thresher)

Log Book film made by ITV 1973.

Log Book film made by KCC film Unit 1975.

School Managers and Education Officer 1961. Mr G. Smith Mr. A. W. Peacock (DEO.). Mrs C. Sunnuchs. Mr W. V. Skinner. Opening of 1961 school extension.

The 'New Maths' 1965. Children using Stern Rods forerunner of Cuisenaire.

Chapter V: 1949 – 1970

As we approach our own time, it becomes harder to be objective. For example after the war there was a controversial scheme for the emergency training of teachers. Through this scheme, the school acquired a teacher in 1948 and, after the brief reign of Alfred Larkin, a headmaster. Those who resented the suspension of normal entrance requirements to the profession, spoke of 'dilution', whilst the friends of the scheme

> *felt that to draw teachers from a wider and more varied field of recruitment might have beneficial results.* [19]

The headmaster in question, D. F. Tye, might have been designed expressly as ammunition for critics of the scheme. He had not passed a single examination, save School Certificate English and History. His teaching experience consisted of six years in an Orpington school – the last three as deputy head. He knew, therefore, something about a very large urban streamed junior school in a very 11 + conscious area, and nothing of the problems of a small village school. He had been able to enter teaching only because of the emergency training scheme which did not demand any academic qualifications apart from the ability to write an essay and interview plausibly: he had written 'a book' about his experiences in the war, and it was probably easier to pass him than to read the book.

It was aptly said of Denis Tye that 'he looks like someone who has been much at sea' and indeed he had served the Navy, in an involuntary capacity; but there remained a distinct streak of cowardice in his makeup. When a boy on a school outing shattered a bottle of lemonade in the nave of Westminster Abbey, the Headmaster took refuge in Poet's Corner.

Otherwise, there is little to be said of his character. As a young man, already thin on top, he wore a suit and was inclined to be 'rather stiff and formal'. An early decision of his was that the school should have a doe for a badge and light and dark blue for sports colours. As the decades wore on, however, he learnt, in the words of the poet, 'to play a true note on a slack string'. That is to say, he could sometimes see a joke and often remember children's names. Much of his efforts went into what he called the 'atmosphere' of the school, although responsibility for heating and ventilation had long since passd to the County Council.

Of his first encounter with the place, he recalls:

When we entered the classroom – so cramped you had to edge sideways down the aisles – the class of juniors sprang to their feet. When they sat down, I was invited to make a few encouraging remarks, at the end of which I asked if there were any questions. After a pause, one boy put his hand up rather timidly, and asked if there would be any football. The smile that crossed all the boys' faces when I replied that of course there would be, is something I'll always remember.

In 1959 he endured the misery of a broken marriage: the school house[20] was never more bleak and the headmaster's study never more distractingly busy than in the next few years.

In the time of this master, somewhat grandiose building projects were conceived, and of the school walls it can be said that he found them green and left them marbled. According to his memory,

The halls used to be bare of any pictures or brightness of any kind. The cupboards were crammed with sets of books mostly of the 1930's (I had to seek permission to destroy a thousand in the first six months). I set to work tidying out the cupboards and in doing so learned the first of my lessons. I expected the staff to be impressed but, to my dismay, found the slight changes I made were met with unspoken disapproval.

Towards the end of his life, whether to identify with the village in which he was not born and the profession for which he was not trained, or whether to distance himself from their trammels, he aspired to the office of local historian, but over this ambition we pass in silence. It is sufficient to relate that some of his friends considered him the Bede of the Village School, and others the Gibbon of Boughton Mounchelsea.

-38-

From 1932 the school had a cleaner and caretaker who used to come to school at 5 a.m. to chop firewood, fill the scuttles and black-lead the grates. The first clerical assistant was appointed in 1946, the first Playground Supervisor in 1955 and the first road crossing patrol in 1960. 'Non-teaching' staff are too often casually neglected in the records, and I will mention two of them from my own time. One, George Brooker the caretaker, actually did some teaching, for he was appointed in 1944 on the strength of the garden and he was soon the only gardening instructor.

An explosion in the Navy in the First World War had left him stone deaf: we communicated by sign language, and he could lip-read. When he spoke or wrote, it seemed that the explosion had stranded him in the speech patterns, as well as the courtesy and perhaps the deference, of 1916. This is from one of his thank you notes:

> *I Glory in your Pluck and the Interest you have taken in the School on different attractions and improvements. I Hope you succeed with all Matters and they are Finally Carried out. But oh Words we have spoken of and what we Receive still seem a Long Way off. But howsoever there is no Harm in trying to improve matters.*

He always dressed the same; a cloth cap, white shirt and tie, sleeveless pullover, grey flannel trousers and black shoes.

> *I used to spend all my school holidays working with him in the school gardens. He was a marvellous man – the patience! – for hours he used to teach me 'Not this way, but that way'. I could understand him well and he understood me. That was the time we had team garden plots, read, green, blue and yellow and he used to*

judge our plots. We used to do experiments with half a potato or the eye of a potato and things like that and of course we could buy the lettuce we grew for a penny each.

He always smoked Players and he'd send me down to the Top Shop, which was Sterry's then, to buy them.

(Robert Thorneycroft)

The second caretaker I remember so well is Reg Copper who was apprenticed to a builder in the days when as an apprentice you learnt every building skill; he was forced to leave a local builders after nineteen years because his bronchitis made outside work impossible.

I knew nothing of the work and my predecessor instructed me only briefly on the basic dutied of the job. I soon found that there was more to it than that, for to have a smoothly running school and to keep it nicely ticking over one must have the co-operation of everyone concerned. This, I think, I succeeded in doing. Of course there were fleeting moments of troubled waters but they soon passed into calm again. In nearly every case the teachers were very friendly and sympathetic to my problems; also patient; I marvelled at their patience and long-suffering which only dedication and love for children can produce.

Before I started at the school, having no children of my own, I did not take much notice of, or have very much to do with, children, and had never been very close as friends to very many. But now they were all around me, so I studied them, and, to some extent, got into their world and found it both enchanting and sometimes startling. I grew to understand and love all children and counted myself lucky at having such an exceptionally good crowd of them at this school. School life taught **me** *a lot, as well as teaching the children.*

(Reg Copper)

-39-

The most decisive change in the relation of school to society since the war, has been the opening of the school to the village and

[112]

especially to that 'co-operation with parents' about which Rolfe had been so sarcastic in 1865.

> *There was, in my early days as School Manager and parent, from 1950, very little communication between the parent and the school; that is something that came quite a lot later. In the early years of my time, parents didn't expect information; they didn't feel shut out but felt, very often, their children weren't getting the treatment they felt they ought to be getting. But they had no means of expressing it, apart from going to a School Manager. They did this, yes but it was second-hand, for if you did take up their points the parents most probably would still think it hadn't been properly dealt with, because they didn't have first-hand explanations.*
>
> **(Gordon Smith,** *interviewed 1979***)**

We can sketch three phases in the opening up of the school. In the first, up until the 1920's the school ventured outside only occasionally, and parents seldom passed through the gates. An excursion is recorded for 1874:

> *The Master, two pupil teachers and 78 children all thoroughly enjoyed the day and with the exception of one or two over-fatigued headaches everything was a success.*

But the next such headaches were not to be inflicted until 1923:

> *School closed on Whit Monday and Tuesday for visit of thirty children to the British Empire Exhibition.*

From then to the war, classes visited the Zoo, Maidstone Museum, **A Midsummer Night's Dream** and, in one over-fatiguing day in 1936,

> *Staff took 39 children to London. Places visited: Houses of Parliament, Horse Guards (Changing of Guard), Westminster Abbey, The Tower, the Zoo and Madame Tussauds.*

Generally, however, the attitude of the school towards the outside world can be summed up by this 1929 entry:

[113]

Wireless lessons have been introduced this week. This has made changes in the Time-Table necessary.

That is to say, the development was perceived not so much in its possibilities as for its disturbance of routine.

In the second phase, from 1923-1948, trips are more frequent and the school is more active in the community. In 1937, there was the first 'Open Afternoon', with speeches and presentations:

Maypole dancing and gymnastics took place on the lawn and the children took the visitors round the garden to show their work.

But the gates were opening mainly outwards:

If parents came up to school it was for a jolly good reason; because you'd been in trouble, or something like that. They very seldom came.

(Pam Thresher)

The 'Open Afternoon' was not repeated, and as late as 1951 we find in the Managers' Minutes that

In reply to a question from Mr. Gordon Smith, the Headmaster, Mr. Larkin, stated that he was not altogether in favour of Open Days – but he had in mind arranging a function of this kind in the winter.

Apart from Athletics, the school activity that linked the school and the village most closely was the Annual Concert. This was held in the Village Hall, which had been built after the First World War as a Memorial. After 1956, the concerts transferred to the school until the new village hall was built in 1978. These events of course brought goodwill to the school and happy anecdotes about them are abundant:

At another time Sally was the Virgin Mary and you and I and Mrs. Nash were sitting at the back of the church. Sally had learned the whole thing, right through; everybody's words. Well, they came on and said their piece and sat down but the shepherds were a bit late

[114]

coming on, so she beckoned them on the pointed to where they'd got to stand. Now the Angel Gabriel – it was Chris Fenner – and I can't remember what he had to say but he'd got to stand up and put his arms straight up in the air. Well, he was saying his piece when Sally realised he hadn't his arms up, so she put the baby in the crib, put his arms up and sat down. And by then I was nearly under the pew.

(Pam Thresher)

A hilarious bit; I don't know which concert it was but I know it was backstage afterwards and no sooner had the curtain gone down but a male angel ripped his halo off and bashed somebody with it. I thought it was marvellous; he just couldn't wait, the aggro had been building up.

(Mrs. Stenning)

I remember being teased because I would be kissed during the final act; in the end the prince couldn't bring himself to do it and ended up by kissing my hand.

(Ann Lamb)

In the third phase, which is still unfolding, not only does the school venture outside, but gradually opens up to parents. The gates swing both ways.[21] Ideally, teachers no longer relate to children while ignoring their parents; but we try to create emotional preconditions for learning in which parents and teachers join in the encouragement of a child's confidence. This means a whole range of regular work, from meetings explaining the curriculum to referrals to the Child Guidance Clinic; but for now the change can again be symbolised by the attitude of special events.

Since the 50's there has been a tendency for these events to reflect something of the life and history of the village, so as to erode the distinctions between learners and public. The very Log Books on which the present essay depends have recently been turned into a video film with the children and neighbours acting the events you have been reading. This notion began in 1965, with

the first school pageant and I think the best and most enjoyable. The idea was to use on old stone out-building as 'gaffers' cottage and then put a false hardboard front on to the canteen wall, painted to re-present one of the new houses in the village. Then gaffer would 'instruct' his commuter neighbour in the history of Kent and Boughton Mochelsea in particular. And so there were scenes repre-senting the ancient Britons and the local iron-age camp; the Roman village at Brishing; and so on down to the first motor-cycle in the village. It was tremendous fun, though not everything went exactly to plan!

(Denis Tye)

One unrehearsed incident was when Dr. Cleaver, the sanitary inspector in 1882, was dusting the Coxheath children, Ian Murdoch, who played the part of Dr. Cleaver got carried away with his tub of flour and not only dusted all the children in sight, but the front row of the parents as well: He had to be restrained.

(Log, 1965)

The first local history exhibition was held in the school in 1968 and attracted enormous local interest. The hall and classrooms were packed with exhibits and the intrepid headmaster slept in the staff-room for their protection. Five hundred visitors, seventy of them ex-hibitors, came to see a marvellous miscellany of bygone tools and utensils, photographs and fossils, scrap books and gardening books, paintings and the Memorial Roll. There was a horse-drawn plough, yoke, flail, butchers' heavy brass scales, milk crock and butter stamp. There were pictures of old buildings and village scenes, of families and school classes, of dramatic and operatic societies; and especially of the traditional occupations: quarry-man, smith, stone-cutter, road-maker, publican, builder. wood-carver, – and fire-work maker.

-40-

The new attitude of the school to the community was carried out in new institutional forms – particularly, the Parents Associaion.

Much help, obviously, was given by parents before this was ever formed. In 1955 the school was seriously deficient in equipment and many of the larger items were bought out of the school fund: a second-hand typewriter, a duplicator, a film projector, and a television set were some of the items bought by money raised at Bring and Buy Sales, Whist Drives, Summer Fair and Concerts. In addition to this kind of help, parents helped with concerts, the Pageant, outings, country dancing and craft work; but at this stage the staff were against help with reading. I instituted regular parent meetings from 1955. Sometimes they took the form of 'Any Questions', with a panel of heads from different secondary schools, a child psychologist, an education officer or the local doctor. Sometimes they were meetings to explain the curriculum.

At these meetings, in 1960 and again in 1961, I raised the idea of an Association:

It was the whole development of the child that mattered and this required the closest co-operation with parents. The headmaster asked for a discussion on whether parents would wish for a Parent-Teacher Association. There was a lively discussion but, finally, the suggestion was overwhelmingly defeated.

(Log)

In 1966, however, during the building of the two new housing estates – totalling about 120 houses, I decided that the school really ought to have a Parents' Association; partly because the scale of activities involving parents made it impossible for me to give enough attention to out-of-school activities without my work in school being affected, especially as until 1969 I was a teaching-head, and partly because I thought positive steps were needed to involve the 'new villagers' with the old. Why I chose a Parents' Association and not a Parent-Teachers' Association, I cannot recall: it was an error of judgement and by 1968 I felt it necessary to change to a Parent-Teacher Association.

Here I am lucky to be able to quote an Open University essay on the Parent-Teacher Association by one of the 'newcomer' parents, Mrs. Maureen Boots. I found her analysis both interesting and rather a shock, as I was not aware at the time of the criticisms she records.

The headmaster of the village school foresaw the possibility of a 'divided' village following the influx of 'newcomers' and therefore envisaged the school's role as introducing a recreational organisation and a meeting point for a fairly large number of village people of widely varying backgrounds, who had at least one thing in common – their children attended the village school. To this end he proposed the formation of a Parents Association; initially he did not wish to be involved in the formal organisation and operation of the society, merely to act as an advisor and to provide the building in which they could meet...

However, despite moderate success and support, by September 1968 the headmaster decided that the Parents Association was not fulfilling his aims and he proposed to the Committee that a Parent/Teacher Association be formed in its place. . . . Despite their personal feelings of disappointment and frustration, the Committee backed the headmaster in his proposals when they were adopted at the Annual General Meeting.

When the Association was only a parental organisation, power decisions rested with the Committee. . . . But even then any matter which directly affected the school had to be referred to the headmaster, who had the power to veto over any decision made, even though he was not a member of the Association.

She then goes on to quote the example of the headmaster vetoing a suggestion that the Association should run an I.T.A. lending library, as it was felt that parents had not enough access I.T.A. books. The essay continues:

It was probably this financial success (i.e. raising £100 at a Summer Fair) coupled with the increasing confidence and authority of the Committee, together with the apparent inability to attract more than a 50% membership (note: parents had to join the Association and pay a membership fee) which led to the change in format of the Association. At this time the headmaster announced plans to build a swimming pool but be was obviously going to need the backing and financial help of the Parents Association. In the society's present form, this could not be guaranteed; there had been some disagreement previously over finance and certainly, both within the membership and on the Committee, there were articulate parents capable of opposing what they regarded as on over-ambitious plan. . .

The headmaster had made a practice of consulting informally with the chairman and secretary; he also kept in very close contact with a number of parents who were not committee members and some were not Association members; he was therefore able to gauge, fairly accurately, the strength of public opinion. There had been a certain amount of bad feeling that the school was being 'taken over' by the 'newcomers'; the committee was also aware of this prejudice and attempted to overcome it without any substantial success; it gave the headmaster the reason he sought to re-vamp the Association. . .

The Association grew up in the wake of the Plowden Report on Primary Education, with its emphasis on the significance of parental participation in school matters. The attempt to harness the advantages of parental interest, by the headmaster, was fairly successful, although the failure to capture a 100% response led to a change in the format. But the success, of those who did participate, held a threat (or was seen to hold a threat) to the authority of the headmaster. Left unhindered the Association and, in particular, the Committee, could have obtained too much power, and it is doubtful if they would have remained silent on school issues with which they disagreed. The third factor/possibility was the undercurrent of criticism from non-members. allowed to continued unchanged, the Association could have resulted in those divisions it was set up to avoid.

The more important reason to my mind, however, for the change to a P.T.A. was the need to unite parents and teachers on the same tasks. I found that not only was the previous Association increasing tensions between the older 'helpers' and the 'newcomers' but it was dividing staff from parents. The formation of P.T.A. did not at first do very much to alter things for, apart from the deputy head, the staff still tended not to participate with sales, fairs, and so on; but the proof of the change came after about 1973 when, largely through the P.T.A., an entirely new relationship grew up between parent and teacher.

To the charge of being authoritarian I plead guilty with the following extenuation. I know of three local schools where the head had devolved much power on parent committees and then fought bitterly against decisions they had made; in two cases the head dissolved the P.T.A. When I formed the P.T.A. I made myself permanent chairman and the deputy head permanent treasurer of the school fund; the secretary was to be a parent and the rest of the committee made up equally of staff and elected parents. The system is now working well: whether a head teacher should have his present general power is another matter. In some areas I think he has too much, and certainly should be more accountable.

-41-

Above all, it was vital to enlist the parents' understanding of curricular developments; and the essay quoted above has already mentioned the most controversial of these – the Initial Teaching Alphabet. As at first sight it would seem to run counter to common sense: there is, of course, a continual need to explain this technique which, for fifteen years now, we have proved successful.

I had the first year juniors before I took the fourth years; most of the children had transferred to traditional orthography by the end of the first half-term; the slower children found the carrot of transferring a great incentive. I cannot remember any children still in i.t.a. by the end of the year.

The great advantages I found was the high standard achieved in all written work; this included spelling, which, I felt, was greatly helped by the children having to look at word structure twice.

The disadvantages were, one, the slight loss of reading experience in the early years from adverts, newspapers and books in the home and, two, the difficulty in sending a child to a t.o. school when half-way through i.t.a.

(Patricia Barrett)

Yes, I remember the parents meeting you held to explain it, and a load were for it, and a load against it, and once again I stood up and said 'We all cribbed about the Cuisenaire rods and it worked; so why not give this a chance and drop it if it's not successful?' My point was that it would help the slower child; these things make no difference to a bright child. It helped the writing a lot because they head only so many sounds to learn – was it 48? – whereas they are over 300 in t.o.? Before that slower children had spent weeks and months in a remedial group.

(Pam Thresher, parent)

Jonathan still claims that i.t.a. is responsible for his bad spelling.

(parent, letter of 1979)

The digging of the swimming pool and the 'adventure playground' are examples of what we could achieve with parents' backing. In the long view, they are also episodes in the ever-shifting negotiations between the school and the country child; for both swimming pool and adventure playground are supervised versions, on school premises, of a relationship to 'nature' that used to be conducted in the farms, woods, streams and illegally entered orchards of the countryside.

John Fuller recalls that in the 1930's

When Harold Waters and a few lads made a swimming pool in Brishing stream I took the children after school for swimming lessons.

I was kept poor because I gave one shilling to everyone when they learned to swim.

The swimming pool was not notified because it would have been considered as grossly unhygienic. However, I think many a Boughtonian learnt to swim there.

(John Fuller, letter of 1979)

The banks were formed by the ragstone removed from the pool. Vic Skinner devised a method of forming a by-pass for the stream and filtering the warmer surface water from it by a system of dams and

[121]

weirs. Help was then offered by the Auxiliary Fire Service Training School, then stationed in Linton Park. Concrete was laid at the bottom of the pool and the banks reinforced. Changing huts, etc. were added and the pool became a very popular spot for family picnics and swimming.

(Peter Barker)

At a later stage, there would be trips to the old Maidstone Baths

with athletes foot and veruccas all over the place; no coat hangers, so your clothes were left on the floor, and a bloke making you put your head under the chlorinated water. The best thing I liked about it was the coach-driver and also the cheese rolls from the tuck-shop after swimming. I really enjoyed a good old cheese roll with your hair all wet and stinking of chlorine and a good old cheese roll to comfort you.

(Kevin Fenner)

Money for the school's own pool was collected from businesses and the parish – and all the digging and concreting was done by a team of fathers. By 1972, we were one of the very few primary schools in Kent who had a heated swimming pool in an enclosed building. With a weekly visit to the new Maidstone Baths for class 1 – not to mention a less military breed of swimming instructors at the baths – swimming has become a pleasure for almost everyone; last year all our fourth year juniors were swimming when they went on to Cornwallis School.

The use of a playground reflects changing philosophies of education. In 1899 we hear of ours getting a new coat of ashes. Through the following decades it was often more of a parade than anything suggestive of play. I described the present version in an article[22]:

We began work in the squelching mud of November 1967 when a group of dads erected an eighteen foot tall gate structure which was sited between a climbing mound with maze, tunnel and sand pit on one side and a 12 foot high amphitheatre, sufficiently large to seat the whole school, on the other. A gravel path led through the gateway to a wooden bridge and a patch of woods beyond. Work proceeded almost without a break on Saturday and Sunday mornings throughout the winter. One of the biggest problems was obtaining enough earth for the mounds and, in desperation, we spent £50 of our precious £175 local authority grant on soil already on site from the building of the new infant block. Work was interrupted at Easter 1968 when we started to erect a swimming pool, which was opened in June. Throughout a hot summer a small group of fathers and I toiled to shape the mounds, pave the large sand pit, slate and path the maze and erect the bridge. The work continued through to the summer of 1969 and one of the hardest jobs was cutting out the steps of the ampitheatre which were retained by old railway sleepers. The playground was opened in June 1969 and has been a tremendous success. Children make woodland camps, climb ropes and play cowboys and Indians in a realistic setting. We have worked out a system of supervision but I hope we do not become too safety minded, for adventure implies legitimate risks.

The school, then, has involved parents in the reading programme where their encouragement to the child is so important, and in practical projects to improve their children's amenities. I hope this co-operation might now extend to a development of the curriculum calling upon skills so many parents possess.

-42-

Such attempts to involve school and community, and the whole compromise between school and countryside which we trace in the last Chapter, now take place within a social structure that since the war has once again changed. As in so many south-eastern villages near large towns, what remains of the old agricultural hierarchy has been overlaid by elements of the commercial-industrial class system – typically, skilled workers in the new council housing, and commuted professionals in renovated 'cottages'. Before the housing estates were built in the early 1960's the first deputy head remembers that

It was a happy school because it was small and the parents connected, because a lot of them had been to the school.

(Catherine Hann)

but that obviously depends upon a stable population. Nowadays, the school must continually renew its claim to co-operation, for both the reliability and the obstacles of the traditional order are dissolving.

In terms of scale, the village has nearly doubled its population since the war, and education had to cope with the post-war 'baby bulge'. After some discussion about hiring the Working Men's Institute, an extension to the school was made in 1960 and again in 1969.

One important index both of the new roles that the school is called upon to play, and also of the social dislocation within which it must now work, is the attention it gives to the significant increase in one-parent families. I have written in an article[23]:

> *This change is all the more noticeable in a village, where the family has hitherto been very stable. Side by side with the quantitative evidence of the increasing toll of divorce and separation, we witness the stress to which children are subjected because of marital strife; temporary separation (it is quite common for mother or father to go away and then return again after some weeks or months); and because of modern open plan houses where children may hear more than they can take. It is not surprising that a larger number of children have behavioural problems and that many more are referred to child guidance clinics. . .*

> *In last term's intake at my school, of the sixteen families no less than four are one-parent. In the current class lists, four or five in each of the six classes have one-parent families. . .*

> *Problems are presented by lack of money, haphazard and insensitive visiting by one of the separated parents, and the social ostracism of many of the mothers. The role of the school is a difficult one and must not be shirked. Classes are too large for the individual attention such children need, and the teacher has to balance the needs of all her class. But it seems to me extremely important that teachers do not make judgements about any parent, and are always ready to listen sympathetically and advise sparingly. Children in such families should be discriminated for and, without sentimentality or the condoning of anti-social behaviour, receive the affection they need.*

The counselling role of the school is now taken very seriously when the parent of a young child dies. Here is an experience from the past that highlights the change:

One of the most vivid things that stands out in my mind regards my school days was the day we were there in Assembly in the big hall. I knew my mother was in hospital but I didn't know she'd actually died and I heard she died in Assembly in Boughton School. and it's rather sad because when I go in that hall now it all comes back to me and very vividly as well.

I can't remember much about my early years at school because through losing my mother this reacted greatly on me and for the first year to two after I didn't get on very well at school, until I went into Miss Longman's class and she sorted me out.

(Mic Fenner)

-43-

The focus of change in the school is the curriculum, and in the next two sections I will compare how it was in 1955 with what it has become since. I arrived to find that not only had the gardening abated, but so had sport and concerts and enthusiasm in general. The old team of teachers had gone, and for a few years there was 'a certain lack of harmony among the school staff' (Managers' Minute, 1950). No curricular innovations are recorded, except that the headmaster's wife took 'eurythmics and dancing'. Perhaps the most significant shifts were the increasing interest in science and use of visual aids.

It was during this period that annual standardised tests were introduced for all the juniors. These tests were in mechanical and problem arithmetic, comprehension, spelling and 'graded word' vocabulary. Kent achieved some notoriety at this time for being one of the most tested counties in the country.

I think both Mr. Fuller and Mr. Larkin were more concerned with the bright children but that was part of the system that operated in those days. Schools were judged by their success in the 11 + or

[125]

scholarship examination.

(Gordon Smith)

The 11 + selection tests were in two parts. The first taken by all the fourth-year junior children in November, took the form of an Intelligence test, preceeded by a practice test and standardized tests in arithmetic and English. From Part 1 a few children went on to sit Part II, in March of the following year, and some of these children might be called for interview at the grammar schools.

During the years 1949-55 few children went on to either the Grammar Schools or the Boys Technical School; entrance to the Girls Technical School did not then take place until 13.

> *My two sons, Alan and Richard, took their exam in Mr. Larkin's day and neither got a good beginning. It was avoidable, absolutely, and not just a question of late development. I think this was one of the main points against the 11 + the result could depend on the headmaster and teachers of that particular primary school how the children did. Both eventually gained good degrees and went on to Wye College. I was lucky in that I could afford to pay to send them to Sutton Valence School.*

(Gordon Smith)

Pressures over the 11 + grew, rather than diminished, as the percentage of 'selected' children grew in the years 1949-1971. Expectations rose as parents became more informed (partly as a result of regular parents' meetings and interviews). No longer did most parents and children assume selective schools were 'not for them'. The official propaganda that every secondary school had a parity of esteem utterly failed to convince parents. It was the middle class rejection of the 11 + that forced in comprehensive schools: for every satisfied middle class parent, there would be more who were not.

> *At the Parents' Meeting, Mr. Chevenix Trench, the Assistant County Education Officer gave a 40 minute survey of the 1944 Education Act as applied to Kent. He spoke at length of the great opportunities in all three forms of secondary schools and emphasised that when mistakes were made in selection they could be put right*

without serious results. He stressed that it was better for a child to be at the top of a modern school rather than to be struggling at the bottom of a grammar school. He emphasised the opportunities in Further Education and explained why Kent had not embarked upon the building of comprehensive schools because that would mean doing away with schools that were flourishing.

After cups of tea, the questions flowed until nine o'clock and it is significant that most of the questions were concerned with the number of Grammar School places in the Maidstone area.

(Log, 1957)

Not all the parents were equally worried but there was a minority who did not disguise their anxiety. In most cases I think parents had confidence in the school but it made for an uncomfortable relationship between parents and staff. This was particularly so after new parents moved into the village when the housing estates were built. I tried to play down the 11 + , but realize now that in doing so I might have been doing some children a dis-service.

I heard you there one night and they were trying to goad you about Loose School getting so many through and I thought you kept your head well. All you said was 'The ones that get through, well, that's not the worry; my worry is about the overall standard of this school and that they're all getting a fair crack of the whip', and that's what I think they do get at Boughton.

(Nigel Fenner)

We were unprepared; there is such a thing as exam strategy.

(Kevin Fenner)

Frank and I were extremely conscious of the 11 + ; we felt that, naturally, we wanted the boys to have 'the best' and the best, to us, was either the grammar school or the technical school. I think I was always very conscious of asking for reports as to how Paul, and the Ian, were getting on.

I was anxious that they should do the best they could. They do say that anxious parents make for anxious children, but on the other hand, I was made that way and that's all there was to it.

Right up until the time we learned Paul had passed, we were anxious and when we had finished with Paul, we started with Ian.

(Mrs. Peggy Brattle)

I remember cases of intelligent children failing to get places because they were shy at interview, and even of one who was afraid to take up the place he had gained.

What did the 'newcomers' to the village feel about the 11 + ? The following letter shows how parents could be torn between approval for a tolerant, liberal education and yet feel the need for competitiveness to bring out the children's best.

My son achieved academic success; his talents were recognised and encouraged but the foundation was laid for a wealth of other interests; he blossomed in an empressured atmosphere. However, his right to present, at times, an uncomformist attitude was respected; he would never, for instance, consent to take a proper part in a school play. On the credit side, this has resulted in a modest young man who remains, and always will remain, his own person. On the debit side, I feel that because he did not experience the pressures of competitiveness, he will take many years to come to terms with any highly stressful situation. But he has already determined he does not want a stressful life and has inner resources within himself.

(Letter from Maureen Boots, 1979))

I thought it would be interesting to see A) what difference the arrival of the new villagers made to the 11 + in terms of selective school passes; and B) what difference was made by selection for the girls technical school at 13 + . Although the estates were filling up from 1965, the impact on the number of leavers did not come until 1970. We then find a jump in the rate of selective places gained, that cannot be wholly accounted for by the increase in numbers seeking places.

A)

	1955-1969	*1970-1971*
Boys going to Grammar School or Sutton Valence (K.C.C. places at an Independent School)	*12*	*3*
Boys to Technical School	*13*	*5*
Girls to Grammar School	*14*	*4*

B)

Girls going to Technical School at 13 +	*19*	*8*

This also shows that when girls had the opportunity to go to Technical School at 13 + they often took this second chance (and went on to do well) – which must cast serious doubt on the possibility of final selection at 11.

-44-

I now come to the test of defining the curricular developments in my own time as head. Until 1971, the 11 + was still in force, but significant changes in national thinking on education had been summarised in the Plowden Report **Children and their Primary School** (1967). Plowden displayed the best practices in primary schools and. influenced by the researches of J.W. Douglas whose **The Home and The School** was published in 1966, emphasised the importance of school-home relationship.

The new thinking of the late 1950's and more strongly the 60's had its origin in the 1920's and 30's. Experiments with infant grouping; the Dalton Plan, which was intended to encourage children to plan their own programmes; the pioneer work of A.S. Neil at Summerhill with maladjusted children; the influence of Susan Isaacs in the field of nursery education **(Intellectual Growth in Children** and **Social Growth in Children** both appeared in the 1930's); the work of Margaret McMillan, also in nursery education; and the researches of Jean Piaget **(Language and Thought of the Child),** were all based on a growing interest in child psychology and child development. The influence of these new ideas was most marked in the infant school, in which field Britain was ahead of the world.

In 1959 I went on a Child Development Course run by the University of London Institute of Education. That year had a profound effect on my views of children and their education. After it I was convinced that a child's educational progress depended on his emotional development and particularly on his own self-regard. Confidence was everything and without it his growth in learning would be stunted. To achieve confidence it was essential that the 'climate' in the school should be caring rather than authoritarian and that there should be the closest co-operation between school and home.

One immediate enemy was corporal punishment, of which Plowden had recommended the abolition:

> *It has been universally outlawed in other western countries. It can be associated with psychological perversion affecting both beater and beaten, and it is ineffective in precisely those cases in which its full use is most hotly defended.*

I inherited the last school punishment book in which was recorded so many strokes of the cane, usually for lying, stealing and bullying – but also for odd offences like 'Putting unwanted food in inkwell holders'. When I first went to the school I caned perhaps three or four boys because it was expected of me and I was weak enough to think that an excuse; I found it degrading, entirely unnecessary and quite ineffective. After the course, I knew it was also morally wrong; I have not used the cane for twenty years or more.

During the 1960's all kinds of developments took place in school organisation to try and meet the new ideas on individual child development: for example, family-grouping, integrated days, and open-plan buildings to enable new groupings of children to be formed. We remained somewhat formal in work structure but became much less formal in relationships with children and parents.

With regard to reading; the introduction of i.t.a. has already been discussed, but before that we put much effort into starting class libraries, encouraging the use of the Kent County Library and changing the reading scheme from Beacon Readers to the new Janet and John infant readers. These the first to be printed in colour were considered at the time to be a great advance. Later I recongised their limitations and with the help of Miss Pitts, a local infant school headmistress, devised a new infant reading scheme which drew upon many different schemes, including some American books – this was the 'platform' approach to learning to read. I then persuaded our staff to abandon group reading – the system whereby groups of infants on the same reading book would sit in a ring and read in turn, 'the speed of the convoy is the speed of the slowest ship'.

Being very keen on art and craft, I encouraged these by extending the range of work in my own class. Hitherto the craft work in this class had been restricted to paper and card handwork.

Boughton School combined with Oldborough Manor School in staging a Handicraft Exhibition in a Marquee at the Boughton Village Fete; Mr. & Mrs. Fuller came to lunch and Mr. & Mrs. Larkin visited us on the afternoon. The Exhibition was regarded as a success, in particular because of the range of activities.

(Log, 1955)

School sports is no less popular today, and the school has notched up some fine results, but the whole affair is much more relaxed. In the early 1960's there was a lot of cricket between schools: now there is very little. Many cricket and football matches between schools were played on Saturday mornings; now this doesn't happen, except at district level and in football where there has been a proliferation of local primary age teams that are run by enthusiastic dads. They have filled the gap left when teachers were no longer willing to give up so much of their free time. In those early years, matches could be unpleasant, with parents protesting at the referee's decision – and not only parents, for I remember a master at a local primary school, who was umpiring a cricket match with me, walking off the field when I gave out one of his team. Today sport is much more good-tempered; at sports days children are no longer made to enter running races and we have seen above that teachers have taken over from the 'sergeant major' swimming baths instructors.

But what of compulsory games for children who hate it?

[131]

Sports Day was something I really hated. My Dad's over-enthusiasm for the thing, I suppose, in a way really killed it for me. He'd say I could play cricket and football well, if I really put myself out, but it never interested me much; I was a rather lethargic little boy. I think it probably really broke his heart, although academic success had very likely righted that. I used to be good at nothing at all – except the egg and spoon race. And, one sports day, I thought I'm really going to win this, but, just before the finishing line, I tripped, in my over-enthusiasm to get to the finish and I fell and no one congratulated me. That, perhaps, is where it all started, and it continued at the Tech where my sports master was like that dreadful archetypal games master in the film **Kes.**

(Kevin Fenner)

I am glad to say that today we are more tolerant and, although each class has team games, and even this can be excused, no one is forced to run races.

Nor, as can be seen from the Adventure Playground, are school games and exercise any longer thought of mainly as organised activities. The Opies, in such books as **Children's Play in Street and Playground** (1969 Oxford) have shown that children have a discipline of fantasy and variation in their own games, which are in some ways more strict than those laid on for them, and which exercise many learning functions including language. Every child remembers

Games in the playgound, which changed according to the latest craze, e.g. skipping games, cat's cradle, peep behind the curtain, sticky toffee.

(Carolyn Harris)

In recording and discussing the children's skipping rhymes, for example, we have shown confidence in the mental work involved. Such 'games' are part of a sub-culture, in which the children transform whatever they are given:

No one liked going up to the school house because it was supposed to be haunted. I remember one day someone said they'd seen a monk at the window, but it was only the reflection of trees.

(Anita Harris)

[132]

Finally, it is a sign of the times that schools now expect or at least seek, rather more consultation with 'the powers that be'.

A year after I arrived, the Divisional Officer told me he knew I would be pleased to learn that Boughton School was not, after all, to be closed. Indeed I was, not having been informed of the threat in the first place. Apparently it had been decided that in the change to larger schools, ours still served an area not easily merged into other schemes.

The school protested against the County Architect's plans for each of the extensions, and in neither case was there proper consultation. In the first, the Architect wanted to fit wash basins in the classrooms instead of with the lavatories. In the second, the siting of a new infant block threatened to cut the school in half, but we were told bluntly that alteration to the plans would risk the building being postponed indefinitely. By chance, I managed to get a staffroom included in the 1960 plans by saving a wood/glass partition from demolition.

The crucial role in such 'negotiations' is, of course, that of the managing body. Under the 1944 Education Act, the local authorities had to compose new managing bodies which would be more representative of the local community. How successful this was can be judged by the fact that thirty years later, the Taylor Report came to entirely different conclusions as to how this should be achieved. Since its recommendations also have been largely ignored, few would think the matter satisfactorily resolved.

Under the 1944 dispensation,

> the managers would have the services of an officer of the local authority as school correspondent.

And so, in a very polite way, the local authority could be 'on the inside' of all managers meetings and make them less independently minded. The effectiveness of the body at that time can be judged from its handling of a series of staffing difficulties:

> We knew there was a lot of trouble on the staff but felt we could do very little about it. Most of us came from middle-class backgrounds

*and knew very little about primary education and we rather left
things to the education officer.*

(Gordon Smith, *appointed School Manager 1952***)**

The slightly altered balance of forces in the 1960's can be
illustrated from the Maidstone plan to set up a three-tier system,
under which Boughton Monchelsea would have become a First
School (5-9) and bus its 9 years olds to the nearby village of
Coxheath. In discussions of the scheme, primary head-teachers were
not invited to the first meeting until I learned of what was happening
and alerted other primary heads, so that, under pressure, the K.E.C.
called a meeting of primary teachers and discovered almost total
opposition.

It remains the case that crucial decisions are usually made in great
secrecy and parents in particular are rarely asked their opinion or, if
they are invited to a token meeting, the decision has already been
made. This is the more to be deplored at a time when there are those
with power in Education who would return us to the 19th century
philosophy of the survival of the wealthiest. We must see that the
hesitant progress of 120 years is not reversed: education is about
social justice or it is nothing.

Invitation to School

I can remember starting school and kids were howling all over the place – it was a terrible trauma. I don't think many children went to nursery school and some parents threatened their children with 'You wait till you get to school', which is like saying 'I'll call a policeman!'

(Susan Brooker *née Lamb***)**

The change in atmosphere between the 1950's and the present is nowhere more apparent than in memories of starting school. What used to be a shock is now eased by the children growing familiar with the place through a playgroup near the school, coming to school on two afternoons in the term before they join, and arriving at staggered times on their first day.

When Marion's boys, Alan and John, and my boy, Guy, started it was completely different. I thought it was marvellous the way you took them in on the first day at ten minute intervals; it made them seem important. And Mrs. Slater said 'Who is going to look after Guy?' and at least three people said 'me'.

(Susan Brooker)

[135]

NOTES

1. **D. F. Tye (ed.), A Village Remembered: Boughton Monchelsea, 1900 - 1940** (Kent Country Library, Maidstone, 1980). Obtainable from the editor at Boughton Monchelsea School, Nr. Maidstone. £2.20 post paid. The present work is an abridged version of my typescript **History of Boughton Monchelsea School, 1850 – 1970** which is filed at the Kent County Library, Springfield, Maidstone.

2. See 'The Use of Oral Sources in History' and 'The Historical Depth of Oral Evidence' in George Ewart Evans' **The Days That We Have Seen** (London, 1975).

3. See D.F. Tye (ed.), **Boughton Monchelsea School: Log Book Extracts, 1863 – 1963** (Boughton Monchelsea, 1976 (1970). Obtainable from Boughton Monchelsea, C.P. School, Nr Maidstone. £1.20 post paid.

4. See, for example, E.W. Gadd, **Victorian Logs** (Studley, 1979).

5. R.F. Geddes, **Queen's Scholarship Examination Questions, 1886 – 1890. With Solutions** (Hull).

6. Pamela Horne, **The Victorian Country Child,** (Adam and Charles Kineton, 1974), p.57.

7. A. Park, **The Higher Education of the Elementary Teachers** (Ashton-under-Lyne, 1889), p.6. The injunction to refrain from 'reflections or opinions of a general character' in the Log Books (see page 9, above) was closely adhered to at Boughton, or we might have more information as to how such attitudes were sustained at school level. In other places, the teachers commented more freely: at Bramshaw in Hampshire, for example, it was announced that

    as the children are of the lowest order, Mrs. Doyley does not admit of any fine work, writing, or anything above their station, lest she should injure both them and the public, by preventing them getting their livelihood in the station wherein they have been placed by

Providence, and thus deprive the community of that class of people who are of such essential consequence to the welfare of the country at large.

(quoted by Elizabeth Merson, **Once There Was The Village School** (Southampton, 1979), p.8.).

8. John Lawson and Howard Silver, **The Social History of Education In England,** University of London Press (London, 1973), p.334.

   When the 1870 Act was passed there were somewhat over 12,000 certificated teachers, half of them women. Ten years later there were 31,000 and in 1895 the number had risen to 53,000 and the proportion of women had risen to almost three-fifths. In the same period the number of pupil teachers rose from 14,000 to 34,000; from just over 1,000 the number of adult assistant teachers rose to 28,000 by 1895

9. M.E. Sadler and J.W. Edwards, 'Public Elementary Education in England and Wales', in **Special Reports on Educational Subjects, 1896-7** (London, 1897), p. 60.

10. **Minutes of the Committee in Council** (1846), II, p. 545.

11. The principal of St. Mark's College, where he trained, was the Reverend Derwent Coleridge, son of the poet. This Coleridge maintained that teacher – training was not for functionaries, but 'to nurture educated and cultured persons'.

12. H.C. Barnard, **History of English Education** (London, 1961 (1947)), p. 293.

13. Defaulters from before 1891 were, however, still being threatened with prosecution.

14. For children between 10 and 12 there was a minimum of 250 attendances, for over 12's a minimum of 150.

15. *We had Arithmetic, English (which included poetry, recitation, spelling, handwriting and dictation) History and Geography. We*

had no Science; Nature Study is the nearest we came to that, and Singing. The girls had needlework and the boys gardening. We did have painting but not a lot until Mr. Smart come to the school. I remember he taught us perspective. **(Ena Potter)**

16. In 1952, the kitchen was closed and meals fetched from Oldborough Manor School.

17. There was a proposal for a new central school at Coxheath, and the Managers agreed
    that the Correspondent write to the Board of Education opposing this scheme on the grounds of being too far from the Parish.
    (Minutes)

18. In 1940, two went to grammar school and one to technical school; in 1941 three went to grammar and one to a county school, and in 1945 four went to grammar and one to an independent school; whereas three went on to grammar schools in 1946, four in 1947, and two in 1948, (together with one free and one fee-paying place at independent school).

19. Barnard, cited in note 12 above, p.304.

20. Since 1961, the master's house has been used as offices, store rooms and archives.

21. To some minds, it could be ominous that one night in 1979 the school gates were stolen altogether.

22. 'A Playground Adventure' in **Art and Craft** (Number 163), special number on the school environment, August 1971. Photocopies from Denis Tye, Boughton Monchelsea C.P. School, Nr. Maidstone. 25p post free.

23. 'Society, Family Breakdown & The School' in **Floating Bridge** (Southampton), February 1977. Photocopies from Denis Tye, Boughton Monchelsea C.P. School, Nr. Maidstone. 25p post free.
    At the end of the day we said a little prayer and lifted our chairs on to the tables; I can hear the scraping and banging that caused at this moment.
    (Susan Hoad)